VISUAL GUIDE TO THE PALACE THAT HOLDS SPAIN'S HISTORY

Royal Alcazar of Seville

TEXTS: RICARD REGÀS **/ PHOTOGRAPHS:** CARLOS GIORDANO & NICOLÁS PALMISANO

D0368446

DOSde**arte** EDICIONES

01

02

contents

01

THE HISTORY OF THE ROYAL ALCAZAR OF SEVILLE

SEVILLE AND THE ALCAZAR

A palace and a city

A thousand years of art and history superimpose within a fortress designed to protect a strategic enclave.

Since its foundation, the evolution of Seville has been bound to the River Guadalquivir. Its political and demographic supremacy in many periods of history was to a large extent due to its situation on the last navigable point of the river for vessels of a certain draft. This is how, the Seville of the Iberians, called *Ispal,* which got to know the flourishing civilization of Tartessos around 700 BC, converted into the *Hispalis* of the Romans in 200 BC –two great emperors, Trajan and Hadrian, were born in neighbouring Itálica– and later into Muslim *Isbiliya,* as a result of the Arab invasion of the peninsular in 711 AD. In the 11th century, the city's destiny remained united forever to the Alcazar, a fortress that was designed to protect the town on the banks of the Guadalquivir, and to hold the residence of the Muslim king and the administrative sections of the capital of the kingdom of *taifas* (emirates). From then on, Seville and its royal palace evolved in unison, sensitive to the intervention of each one of the monarchs that lived within its walls who in the majority of cases greatly admired what their predecessors had constructed. The building complex that combines remains from all periods, from the Caliphate of Cordova up until now, and whose walls have witnessed great events in Spanish history can still be admired today.

Portico of Palace of Peter I

The Muslim Alcazar

From fortress to palace during two centuries of extensions

The Caliphate of Cordova, in the 10th century, was a period of great splendour for Muslim dominion on the Iberian Peninsula. Its decomposition, in the 11th century, led to diverse kingdoms called *taifas*. One of them, Seville, converted into the capital of Al-Andalus. The new royal court meant that a great palace, the *Alcázar Bendito* was necessary, which the Almohads, in the 12th century extended and enriched.

From Cordova to Seville

In 929, the Emir of Cordova Abd al-Rahmán III cut all ties with Baghdad and proclaimed himself Caliph. For one century, Cordova is capital of Al-Andalus and Seville occupies a servile position, provided with a small fortress –the so-called Governor's House– possibly set up in the current location of the Alcazar. The collapse of the caliphate and the emergence of the *taifa* of Seville, which in a few decades goes on to dominate a good part of Al-Andalus, inverts the relationship between both cities.

Abd al-Rahmán III
Made Al-Andalus independent from Baghdad.

¿WHAT IS AL-ANDALUS?
It was the territory on the Iberian Peninsula under Muslim control.

CHRISTIANS

MUSLIMS

Muslims on the Peninsula
The kingdom of Abd al-Rahmán III (10th century) is the zenith of Muslim power.

THE ALCAZAR'S EXTENSIONS

11th Century
The Blessed Alcazar
The original palace took up what was later the House of Trade and Peter I's Palace.

Original wall

12th century
The Almohad Alcazar
The walls of the palace practically reach their present dimensions.

Al-Mutamid
A lover of poetry, he led the taifa kingdom of Seville to dominate a large part of Al-Andalus and started a period of great cultural splendour.

Poetry book

The Blessed Alcazar

Throughout the 11th century, the taifa kingdom of Seville combined great military and political power. The position as capital of a vast territory required the construction of a palace that would house the Court of the new Abadí dynasty. To this end, the taifa king of Seville Al-Mutamid (1040-1095), or rather his father and predecessor Al-Mutamid (1000-1069), had the *Alcázar Bendito* (al-qasr as-Mubarak) constructed in the sector now taking up the Admiral's Room and King Peter's palace. The most admired room of the residence of the Sevillian taifa kings was a Throne Room on whose cupola are the Pleiades, a star cluster used to decorate meeting areas.

The Stucco Patio
Built at the end of the C20th and main trace of the Almohad Alcazar.

>>>
The Gold Tower
The Almohads raised this bastion in 1221.

1147
IS THE YEAR
when the Almohads, a Moroccan caste that tried to return to the origins of Islam, invaded the Peninsula and joined it to the capital of Seville.

>>>
The Giralda
The tower of the mosque of Seville dates from 1198.

The Almohads

In the 12th and 13th centuries, the Almohads carried out great works in the Alcazar, whose walls were stretched to their present boundaries. Of the same era are the *qubba* of the garden (now Charles V Dining Room), the Stucco Patio and the old Crossing Courtyard, whose two levels –an upper walkway supported by vaults that shelter a pool– provoked great admiration.

CHRONOLOGY
IMPORTANT FACTS ABOUT THE PERIOD

712
Muslim conquest
The soldier of Yemeni origin Musa ibn Nusair snatches Seville away from the Visigoths.

1078
Maximum extension of the taifa of Seville
In 1031, the Caliphate of Cordova is divided into many kingdoms.

1172
Seville's great mosque
It was constructed on the present site of the cathedral.

The Gothic Alcazar

The construction of the palace of Alfonso X the Wise

Recently abandoned by the last Almohad caliph, the Alcazar of Seville captivated Ferdinand III, the Christian king that conquered the city, and his successor, Alfonso X, for an architectonic and decorative richness whose exuberance contrasted with the austerity of Christian castles. For this reason, the Alcazar converted into one of the regular residences of the Kings of Castile and, later, the Spanish monarchs.

Cultural superiority

Ferdinand III and his heir, Alfonso X, were both more than aware of the cultural superiority of their opponents. For this reason, after occupying Seville, they respected the conquered patrimony and enjoyed it up to the point that both decided to die within the walls of the Alcazar. Alfonso X gathered together his entourage of scholars –which King Al-Mutamid had also done in the same place centuries before– and there wrote many of the essays and poems that earned him the title of Wise.

Alfonso X the Wise
King of Castile from 1252 to 1284, his military determination against the Muslims contrasts with the foundation, in Toledo, of the School of Translators, example of intercultural concord.

1248
IS THE YEAR
when Ferdinand III takes Seville off Muslim hands and converts the city into the capital of his court, along with Toledo, and the Alcazar into a royal palace.

The Reconquest after Alfonso X
Only the Nasrid kingdom of Granada resisted Castilian troops.

THE ALCAZAR'S EXTENSIONS

1254
Gothic style
King Alfonso X the Wise had his royal residence built in the Gothic style inside the Muslim Alcazar, on the remains of the Almohad palace, next to the Crossing Courtyard.

Gothic palace

The wise king
Although he was a great promoter of Castellano as a language of culture, Alfonso X composed his poems in Galician- Portuguese, for example the *Cantigas de Santa María*.

The Gothic Palace. it is the main vestige of the intervention of Alfonso X in the Alcazar, though its rooms are also known as Charles V's rooms because the tiles and the tapestries that decorate them pay homage to the emperor.

Gothic symbolism

Despite his admiration for Andalusian architecture, Alfonso X preferred to build a residence of new ground plan in an area of the Alcazar situated next to the Crossing Courtyard, constructed by the Almohads. In order to symbolize the triumph of Christianity, the king wanted the palace to be of Gothic style. He contracted the stonemasons of Burgos Cathedral, who planned a building of rectangular shape, with 4 towers on the corners, a sober façade and a terrace roof that was to be used as a parade ground. In the end, Alfonso X had the Almohad patio's pool covered over with cross vaults in order to create the underground garden that today constitutes the Baths of María Padilla.

The capture of Cadiz. With the conquest of this city in 1262, Alfonso X's troops arrive at the Atlantic.

 CHRONOLOGY
IMPORTANT FACTS ABOUT THE PERIOD

1236
The Conquest of Cordova
Ferdinand III's troops enter in the old capital of the Andalusian caliphate.

1239
Construction of the Alhambra
The first king of the Nasrid dynasty orders work to be started on the Alcazar of Granada.

1264
Mudejar uprising
Alfonso X confronts a Muslim soldier rebellion.

The Mudejar Alcazar

Muslim art for Christian monarchs

The construction of the palace of the Alhambra in the neighbouring Muslim kingdom of Granada wielded great influence on the tastes of the Kings of Castile. During the 14th century, two monarchs, Alfonso XI and his successor, Peter I, lured many Moorish artisans to the Seville court in order to reconstruct the Alcazar in Mudejar style, the art that combined constructive elements of Christian and Muslim traditions.

Internal fighting

From the reign of Alfonso X in the mid 13th century, the map of the Christian conquests on the Peninsula remained almost unchanged for more than 2 centuries. The internal struggles between nobles and kings, and the wars between mainland Christian kingdoms obliged successive Castilian monarchs to use reserves of money that in other circumstances would have been ploughed into the conquest. The case of Peter I (1334-1369) is paradigmatic: he confronted the neighbouring kingdom of Aragon and spent his entire life thwarting conspiracies –the nickname *Cruel* is due to the great number of rivals that he had assassinated– and on many occasions sought help from the Granadan Muslim King.

The Hall of Justice

Next to the Stucco Patio, it is the first Mudejar work of the Alcazar and of Seville. Alfonso XI had it built from 1340 after winning the Battle of Salado.

María of Padilla
Lover of Peter I –who had 2 legitimate wives–, her influence was felt in the Sevillian court. On her death she was declared Queen.

King Peter's Palace

Monarch since the age of 15, Peter I spent most of his childhood in the Alcazar and grew up in a climate of tolerance towards Muslims and Jews. In 1364 he brought together the best artists from Granada, carpenters from Toledo and masters of Sevillian works –almost all Muslims– in order to construct his palace in the Alcazar. This is how the royal residence of Peter I is a compendium of the best of Islamic art on the Peninsula, including models from the Alhambra of Granada, the Cordova under the Caliphs and Jewish-Mudejar Toledo. Peter I, however, could hardly enjoy the palace, as he was assassinated in 1369, aged 34.

Peter I the Cruel
During his reign he had his father's lover assassinated and six of his step brothers. Only one, Enrique de Trastámara, remained alive, and it was he who killed the king in a hand-to-hand combat, converting into his successor.

18
YEARS OF AGE
was Peter I when he married Blanca de Borbón, who he then abandoned two days later.

<<<
The Maidens' Patio
Peter's Palace goes around this beautiful patio.

Castile and León shield
The symbols of both kingdoms joined under a sole crown are repeated in the Alcazar.

Gold coin
The *dobla de oro* was the currency of Castile minted in Seville between 1350 and 1365 with the effigy of Peter I.

Multiculturalism. On the portico of King Peter's Palace are phrases in Arabic (blue) and in Castellano (black).

CHRONOLOGY
IMPORTANT FACTS ABOUT THE PERIOD

1340
Battle of Salado
Alfonso XI conquers the Benemerines, the last north African dynasty that tried to invade the Peninsula.

1348
The Black Plague
A pandemic of bubonic plague decimated the population throughout Europe and killed King Alfonso XI in 1350.

1391
Assault on the Jewish Quarter
4,000 Jews assassinated in Seville after an anti-Semite manifesto.

The Renaissance Alcazar

The palace becomes headquarters for trade with America

The Catholic Monarchs ended two centuries of anarchy, stagnation and conflicts between the Crown and nobility with the dynastic union of Castile and Aragon, the conquest of the Nasrid kingdom of Granada –last Arab stronghold on the Peninsula– and the economic support to the expedition of Columbus to America, which allowed Castile to conquer the continent and transformed Seville into the capital of an empire.

Seville, capital of the world

Assiduous residents of the Alcazar of Seville, Isabella I of Castile and Ferdinand II of Aragon chose the city, and the royal palace as headquarters for the House of Trade, the body created in 1503 to promote and regulate trade with colonized America. To this end, they built on the site where in the past was located part of the *Alcazar Bendito* of Al-Mutamid. With this decision, Seville achieved the monopoly and its golden age.

Seville, in the 16th century
Work of Alonso Sánchez Coello that is found in the Museum of America, in Madrid.

1526

IS THE YEAR when Charles V –Charles I of Spain– gets married in the Alcazar to Isabella of Portugal.

The Spanish Empire, after annexing Portugal in 1580

THE ALCAZAR'S EXTENSIONS

1503
The Upper Palace
Apart from constructing the House of Trade, the Catholic Monarchs carried out extense alterations to improve the habitability of the Upper Palace, the winter royal residence.

Upper Palace

Christopher Columbus
On October 12th of 1492, he set foot on American soil in an expedition paid by the Kingdom of Castile.

Santa María ship

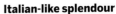

The Admiral's Quarters
Façade of the old headquarters of the House of Trade, created by the Catholic Monarchs to regulate trade with America and provide classes of cartography and navigation.

Italian-like splendour

In the 16th century, during Charles V and Philip II's reign, Spain underwent a period of great splendour. In the Alcazar, the gold from America led to sumptuous renovations, almost all carried out in Renaissance style: semi-circular arches and Ionic and Corinthian columns carved in marble from Carrara by Genoese sculptors stand out in the Upper Palace. Now under the declining Philip III, at the start of the 17th century, the Milanese architect Vermondo Resta completes this Italian slant by transforming former Muslim gardens into Mannerist style gardens.

Spain and Portugal
The shield of Spain under Philip II includes the symbols of Portugal, annexed to the Spanish crown between 1581 and 1640.

Philip II
King from 1556 to 1598, he led the first global empire.

 CHRONOLOGY
IMPORTANT FACTS ABOUT THE PERIOD

1479
Dynastic union
Isabella I and Ferdinand II attained the union of Castile and Aragon, the Peninsula's most powerful kingdoms.

1492
Conquest of Granada
The Catholic Monarchs take the capital of the last Muslim kingdom on the Peninsula.

1609
The Expulsion of the Moors
In 1492 the Jewish population had already been exiled from Spain.

The Romantic Alcazar

The first renovations in the Sevillian palace

After a century and a half of decadence for the loss of the monopoly of trade with America (1717), Seville undergoes a new boost in the second half of the 19th century with the arrival of the railways and the destruction of its walls. In this atmosphere of recaptured optimism, the taste for nineteenth century Romanticism by recuperating the glorious past involves the first works of restoration of the Alcazar.

The restoration work

Romanticism arrived late to Spain but gathered force in the city of Seville, personified in the figure of a poet named Gustavo Adolfo Bécquer. One of the features of this movement is the recuperation of the past as a method of national affirmation. In the artistic world, it is during this period when the classification of historic buildings is systematized according to the style in which they were constructed. Within this context, the Royal Alcazar of Seville –an authentic compendium of the history of Spain and of art– represents a great opportunity for study. It is for this reason that from the year 1832 the first real restorations of the royal palace take place, some of them, however, quite unorthodox.

Alfonso XII
King between 1874 and 1885, he was the first Spanish monarch that was openly liberal –fruit of his education in diverse European capitals– in contrast to the absolutism of his predecessors.

1902
IS THE YEAR
when Alfonso XIII, successor of Alfonso XII, assumes power at the age of 16.

1929
IS THE YEAR
in which the Latin American Exhibition of Seville was held –inaugurated on the 9th of May and closed on the 21st of June the following year– the climax in a period of recuperation for the city.

>>>
English Garden
Carried out in Romantic style.

THE ROYAL ALCAZAR EXTENSIONS

20th Century
The New Gardens
During the reign of Alfonso XIII it was decided to landscape the large extension situated to the north and to the east of the Alcazar, formerly occupied by gardens of the Almohad era.

Gardens

The Marchena Gateway
In 1913, King Alfonso XIII acquired at auction the Gothic portal of the Palace of the Dukes of Arcos, situated in Marchena, and he had it brought to the Alcazar.

English Garden. It presents a scenic style that contrasts with the geometric order and the fragmentation dominant in the rest of the gardens of the Alcazar planned in their majority at the start of the 17th century in Mannerist style.

The New Gardens

The gardens were exalted as *nature humanized* for their romanticism. That's why it was at this time, at the start of the 20th century, when the New Gardens were designed on the former Muslim orchards of the Alcove (*Alcoba*) and the Retreat. The so-called English Garden, paradigm of the romantic orchard, extends to the eastern and southern walls of the Alcazar. It paid homage to British Victoria Eugenia of Battenberg, wife of Alfonso XIII and Queen Consort of Spain. The Garden of Retreat, which occupies the most northern sector of the Alcazar, was planned from 1913 to 1917, while the Poets' Garden, located between the two just quoted, wasn't designed until 1956.

Isabella II
Queen of Spain from 1833 to 1868, handed over the Alcazar as residence to the Dukes of Montpensier.

Neo-Mudejar
Mudejar shapes were recuperated in works such as the Hotel Alfonso XIII (photo) and Cordova station.

CHRONOLOGY
IMPORTANT FACTS ABOUT THE PERIOD

1812
Liberal constitution
Reunited in Cadiz, Spanish Parliament set out the first Spanish Magna Carta.

1839
Excavations in Itálica
The restoration of the Roman city near Seville begins after many centuries of pillaging.

1898
Cuba War
Spain loses a great part of what remained of her far-reaching colonial empire.

02

The Royal Alcazar of Seville

A palace of Muslim origin with ten centuries of history

Due to its Muslim roots and its evolution during ten centuries of use as royal residence, the configuration of the Alcazar is at odds with the concept of the traditional castle-palace in European culture of Christian origin, given that it tends to the fragmentation of spaces, clearly distinguishes public and private areas, and generates rooms of relatively small dimensions whether in surface area or in height.

Intimate architecture

As opposed to the model of Romanesque castle-palace, Gothic or Renaissance style, characterized by their simple organization, their spacious and lofty rooms and the importance of the façade as a decorative element, the Alcazar is structured around various patios, some for public use and others residential. Moreover, in general it presents spaces that are very fragmented –to guarantee habitability and privacy–, its rooms are constructed on just one level or at the most two, and reserves the decorative works for the interior instead of displaying them, like the Christians, on the outer walls, hence the strict sobriety of the Alcazar's outer walls.

1254
THE YEAR in which Alfonso X has the Gothic Palace constructed, first Christian work in the Alcazar

Maze of patios and rooms
Different sized patios connect and provide light to the disjointed arrangement of palace rooms.

The Flag Square

6,5
HECTARES is the surface area that the Royal Alcazar and its gardens occupy.

Tower

Access to the Flag Square

Almohad wall

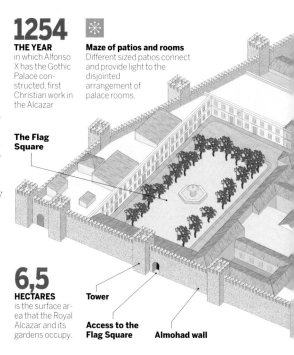

Hall of Justice. Built by Alfonso XI halfway through the 14th century and the first Mudejar work in the palace.

Stucco Patio. Planned at the end of the 12th century, it is a great vestige from the Almohad period.

The Hunting Courtyard. Area created in the 14th century, during the construction of the King Peter's Palace.

Crossing Courtyard
Of Almohad origin (12th century), it was totally transformed in the era of Alfonso X (13th century) and after the Lisbon earthquake of 1755.

Gothic Palace
Alfonso X, second Christian king that lived in the Alcazar, had a Gothic style palace constructed within its walls to symbolize the triumph of Christianity.

Lantern of the Gothic Palace

The Galley Garden

Modern Patios

The former House of Trade

1364
IS THE YEAR
when work commences on Peter I's palace.

Lion's Courtyard

The Lion Gateway

Peter I's Palace
The monarch has his royal residence built in the Mudejar style in an area of the Alcazar that was formerly occupied by the Muslim palace

The heart of the city

Despite the fact that its original nucleus was constructed outside the city, outside its walls, the Alcazar nonetheless had a lot of influence on Seville's public life, with which a large area –around seven hectares, similar to various football pitches– appears surrounded by the main Medieval and modern buildings of the period, such as the Cathedral, the Exchange (now the Archive of America), the Royal Manufacturer of Tobacco (now the University) or the Hospital of the Venerable.

The walls

Solid sections of walls of great sobriety protect the Alcazar and hide its riches and wealth within.

Ancient walls

Defined as "impregnable" by a Muslim poet of the 11th century, the Alcazar walls carried on expanding as the palace grew in surface area parting from the palace of the Sevillian taifa kings, the original core of the fortress. Dating from this first period are two stretches of wall that form the outer angle of the Flag Square: the one that goes round Victory Square and Joaquín Romero Murube Street, and the one that, starting from that corner arrives at the Water Tower, next to the Marchena Gateway and borders with the Neighbourhood of Santa Cruz. As opposed to what happened to the majority of the city's walls, the ancient walls of the Alcazar were saved from demolishment in the year 1868.

Alcorizan stone
The material used in the construction of the walls comes from the neighbouring province of Los Alcores. It is called calcarenite and is a type of limestone.

99
METRES
measures the original wall from the 11th century in Victory Square and Romero Murube Street.

Brick pattern
The bonding alternates with bricks juxtaposed on their longer side and shorter sides.

Crenellations
They were positioned high on the ancient wall in the reign of the Almohads, in the 12th century.

Irregular masonry

NOTE
SEVILLE'S WALLS

Although at first they were separate, the Alcazar's walls and those of the city ended up joining together in the C12th, under the reign of the Almohads. A wall originating from the Alcazar arrived at the Guadalquivir crossing the Abd al-Aziz, the Silver and Gold Towers, the latter located next to the river bank.

7,3
KILOMETRES
is the perimeter of Seville's walls before their demolishment in 1868. They had 166 towers, 13 gateways and six side doors.

Gold tower

Walled perimeter
between the 12th and 19th centuries Seville was probably the best defended city in Europe.

**<<
Diamond
point**
The characteristic decorative ending can be seen in many fortresses in Spain and Morocco.

Column
One of the towers that flanks the Lion Gateway has a carved column that dates from the Alcazar's Muslim period.

LOCATION

Walls and towers

Raised to defend the palace structure of the Alcazar similar to a citadel, the solid walls measure two metres thick and are comprised of three layers of stone ashlars that are placed in irregular form. The towers, high and narrow, alternate brickwork with stonework. It is quite probable that a large quantity of the ashlars that are used originate from walls and constructions from Roman times.

Ceramic work from the 19th century

Tower

Lion Gateway

Fawn

11th century doorway
On the street named Joaquín Romero Murube, near the Flag Square.

Silver archway
The main entrance to the *Alcázar Bendito* in the taifa period, in the C11th.

Tower of Abd al-Aziz
It connected the defensive stretch of the Alcazar with the Silver Tower.

The Silver Tower
A halfway observation point between the Guadalquivir and the Alcazar.

The entranceways

The subsequent extensions of the Alcazar over a period of ten centuries have brought about different entranceways.

The Lion Gateway

Called the Hunting Gateway up until the 19th century for leading into the courtyard with the same name, the main entrance of the Alcazar was re-baptized due to the putting in place, in 1894, of a panel of tiles that, over its arch, show a heraldic lion with a crown and a cross, standing on a flag. Although originally it was to be a horseshoe shaped archway, the doorway is a semi-circular arch framed in a discreet bas-relief. It became the main entrance to the Alcazar after the construction of Peter I's palace, in the 14th century. The stretch of wall on which it is found, whitewashed and painted red, belongs to the original walls of the Alcazar, built in the 11th century by Al-Mutamid or his predecessor.

The Lion's Courtyard. It separates the gateway of the same name and the Hunting Courtyard and is dominated by the section of the Alcazar's original wall, on its northern side.

NOTE
FLAG SQUARE

Probable military square of the original nucleus of the Alcazar of the 11th century, the Flag Square hosts after the Christian conquest the ceremonies of recognition of the new kings on behalf of the people of Seville. Originally, in the buildings surrounding it resided the Alcazar's civil servants.

<<<
The Lion
The inscription 'Ad Utrumque' is part of a phrase in Latín that means "Ready to do what is necessary".

1625
IS THE YEAR
of construction of the Hunting Courtyard's *corral*, a great theatre located in the Lion's Courtyard.

Coat of arms
The historian José Gestoso designed a tile with the royal coat of arms for the gateway of the Flag Square.

LOCATION

01. The Lion Gateway

02. Flag Square gateway
The capitals of the interior arch are Almohad, from the 12th century.

03 and 04 Mounting block
Work of Italian architect Vermondo Resta of 1609, the façade of the mounting area has two levels and is considered a masterpiece of Sevillian Mannerism. A crown and tiles with Philip V's coat of arms can also be made out in the decoration.

05. Altarpiece
At the end of the nave, it welcomes visitors arriving by carriage.

The mounting block

At the end of the Flag Square is the entranceway to the mounting area, the entrance to the palace for the carriages. Designed by Milanese Mannerist architect Vermondo Resta between 1607 and 1609, it has a basilica ground plan, with three naves separated by pairs of Tuscan columns that support semi-circular arches and roofs with flat wooden beams. A Baroque altarpiece with the *Presentation of the Virgin in the Temple* decorated the wall at the end. It dates from the latter part of the 17th century and it is made from golden and polychrome carpentry. To the right of this wall is a large corridor parallel to the Crossing Courtyard that leads arrivals through to the Hunting Courtyard, the core of the Alcazar.

Gateway of the New Gardens

THE ALMOHAD ALCAZAR

The Hall of Justice and the Stucco Patio

The Stucco Patio is the only trace of the Almohads' skill in the manufacture of ornaments with this material.

The presence of the Muslims on the Iberian Peninsula lasted 8 centuries, a long enough period to set off very diverse trends within the Islamic world. The emirs and caliphs of Cordoba (the 8th to 10th century) and the taifa kings of Seville (11th century), native of the Arabíga Peninsula, were followed by the Berbers in the 12th century, who came from Morocco. In the 12th century, a Berber caste, the Almohads, created a great empire to the north and south of Gibraltar to recuperate the essence of Islam, believed to be adulterated by their predecessors. For Seville, Almohad dominion was a period of great splendour. The city converted into the capital of the European part of the empire and had a privileged relationship with Marrakech, the main imperial headquarters. This glory was translated into a large number of constructions –the Giralda and the Gold Tower– whose austerity and geometric rigour –basic features of Almohad architecture– can still be admired today. In the Alcazar some decisive interventions were made: walls were extended and what is known by archeologists as the Stucco Patio was constructed and displays a masterly use of this material. This royal residence, located in the northern zone of the original Alcazar, took up areas to the left of the Hunting Courtyard, among which are found the oldest spaces of the Alcazar since its latest refurbishment: the Stucco Patio, Almohad work from the 12th century, and the Hall of Justice, with a structure from the same period and mid 14th century decoration, the first Mudejar work in the palace, two decades before the intervention of Peter I in the palace that is named after him.

Abu Yaqub Yusuf
Almohad leader that led the invasion of the Peninsula in 1170 and then settled in Seville, where he had the Stucco Patio constructed in the Alcazar.

The Hall of Justice

The first Mudejar work in the Alcazar of Seville

In 1340 King Alfonso XI of Castile claims victory in the battle of the River Salado against the Benemerine Dynasty, a Berber caste that tried to conquer the Peninsula. The monarch wanted to celebrate this triumph by rebuilding one of the Almohad areas of the Alcazar in the new Mudejar style, an art that combined constructive and decorative elements of Christian and Muslim origin.

First Mudejar structure

Of cubic configuration, the Hall of Justice was probably a *qubba* of the Almohad palace that Alfonso XI decided to reconstruct midway through the 14th century using, for the first time in Seville, the Mudejar style that would later be the protagonist in the construction of the palace of Peter I. The stuccowork that partially covers the inside of the room with stylized plant motifs and epigraphy –commemorative engravings– is from the same period, as well as the octagonal roof that covers the space, with knotwork inside and on the corners, and a honeycomb pineapple in the centre.

The room
Situated between the Lion's Courtyard and the Stucco Patio, its walls have two strips of Mudejar plasterwork: around the arches and high up, next to the wooden roof.

?

WHAT IS A QUBBA?
It is a construction that the Muslims probably inherited from Persian architecture and which is characterized by its cubic form topped with a cupola in the shape of half an orange.

Coffered ceiling

Upper frieze

Drain

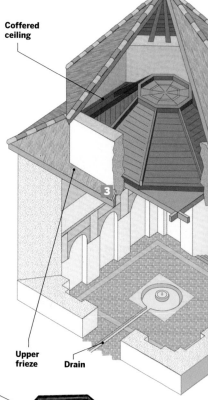

Muqarna
Pineapple detail that decorates the centre of the Mudejar roof.

Lattice work
The upper frieze of the room is made up of latticework and small blind plasterwork arches.

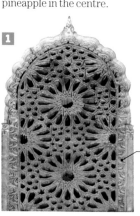

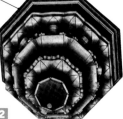

81
METRES SQUARE
is the surface area of the Hall of Justice. Its ground plan is square and measures 9 metres each side.

Plaster detail

Ceramic. Decorative detail.

Fountain. Stucco Patio's drain.

Octagonal base

1358

IS THE YEAR in which Peter I the Cruel assassinates his step-brother and opponent, Don Fadrique, supposedly in the Hall of Justice.

 3

Coats of arms On the upper frieze of the room, shields of the kingdoms of Castile and León can be found, along with Arabic epigraphs.

Coffered ceiling. An octagonal roof covers the room, of square ground plan.

NOTE
THE ENGRAVINGS OF THE ROOM

In Arabic writing and language despite being a commission from the King of Castile, the epigraphs that decorate the walls of the Hall of Justice praise Allah and Peter I, " Lord of the Alcazar". The engravings are of great importance in the Muslim world as Islam bans the representation of people and animals.

The Court of Peter I

Although it acquired its presence appearance during the reign of Alfonso XI (1331-1350), the Hall of Justice was so baptized due to the use it was given by its successor, Peter I the Cruel (1350-1369). who apparently judged the accused –a power of the Medieval kings– from a throne attached to one of the walls of the room.

Stucco Patio

Constructed in the 12th century, it is the only trace of the palace built by the Almohads on the site of the Alcazar.

Decoration
The small lobulated shapes that make up the arches of the portico are developed on further up, in the lattice work.

The most ancient area

The Stucco Patio formed part of the palace baptized with the same name by the archeologists due to the masterly use that the artisans made of this material in order to create their decorative elements. The oldest area in the Alcazar that has reached our times with little moderation, the patio is the last intact vestige of the Almohad period –12th century– and of 200 years as a Muslim palace. Rectangular and with a pond in the centre, it presents an original composition, with the gallery on one of its long sides, which is a link between the Cordovan splendour of the 10th century, depicted in the palace of Medina Azahara, and the architecture of Granada of the 14th and 15th century, represented by the Alhambra.

The patio
The stucco on the porticos is a sample of the decorative restraint of the Almohads, whose genius greatly influenced in Nasrid and Mudejar art.

Horse shoe archway
On the archways of the northeast wing are hollows inspired by the shapes of the Cordova of the Caliphs.

Northeast wing. The triple arcade could date back to before the Almohads, as it follows caliphal models.

Caliphal capital. The columns on the south-east wall suggest the presence of arcades, now disappeared.

Two bedrooms. Two horseshoe arches allow access to a room with couchettes at the far ends.

The capitals
They crown the portico's marble columns and are of caliphal style, inspired by the Cordova of Adb al-Rahmán III, of the 10th century.

LOCATION

?

WHAT IS SEBQA?
It is a type of ornamentation in stucco of typical Almohad style, based on the repetition of geometric and naturalist forms.

170
METRES SQUARE
is the courtyard and gallery area.

The latticework gallery

The portico on the southeast wing, the only trace of Almohad craftsmanship using stuccowork, is composed of three modules. The central one is supported by means of two brick pillars of squared section that hold up a scalloped arch decorated with *sebqa* work. The two lateral modules –identical– include three lobulated arches whose upper walls also show sections of *sebqa*, on this occasion forming latticework.

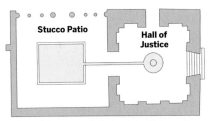

Stucco Patio

Hall of Justice

Water. A drain connects the fountain with the pool.

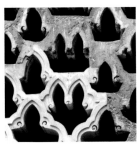

'Sebqa'. Detail of stuccowork of the Almohad ceilings in one of the lateral modules of the portico.

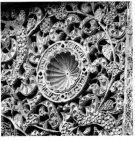

Stucco. Close-up of decoration in the arch that connects the Stucco Patio with the Hall of Justice.

The pool. Surrounded by a hedge, it occupies the centre of the patio and a good part of the area.

THE HOUSE OF TRADE

The Hunting Courtyard and Admiral's Quarters

For two centuries, the Spanish Empire was governed from the salons that open on to the neuralgic centre of the Alcazar.

In parallel to the construction, between 1364 and 1366, of the palace of King Peter, a vast area was opened up where until that time the former residence of the taifa kings of Seville had been located, constructed three centuries before. This space, of trapezoidal shape and presided by the spectacular Mudejar portico of the Palace of Peter I, very quickly turned into the meeting point of noblemen for the hunts that were organized by the Spanish kings, hence the name the Hunting Courtyard (*Patio de la Montería*). At the beginning of the 16th century, with the Catholic Monarchs' foundation of the House of Trade for America (*La Casa de Contratación de Indias*) the courtyard became the Alcazar's epicentre, the place around which are structured the majority of the complex's rooms. The House of Trade, which in 1503 occupied the western side of the Hunting Courtyard, was created in order to control commercial movements with America whose colonization had started a mere eleven years before. In that way, these buildings within the Royal Alcazar were transformed, over a period of two centuries, into the logistical centre of the first global empire in the history of Mankind, an immense task that included the control of American merchandise that arrived at the Sevillian port in the way of monopoly, the establishment of laws that regulated such trade, the training of navigators to guide the sailing vessels across the oceans and the training of cartographers –such as Américo Vespucio or Juan de la Cosa– who recorded the coordinates and layout of explored lands.

Isabella I of Castile
Her visionary intuition to support the first voyage of Christopher Columbus allowed the Crown of Castile to create an intercontinental empire during the sixteenth century.

The Hunting Courtyard
The neuralgic centre of the Alcazar

Product of Muslim taste for atriums –cloisters that provided access to Roman houses–, the Alcazar has no less than ten courtyards of uneven layout, result of their evolution over one thousand years. The Hunting Courtyard, already constructed in the Christian period, is the most important, as it acts as the centre from which all the palace's main buildings can be reached.

Four wings
Of trapezoidal shape and aesthetically marked by the Mudejar façade of the Palace of Peter I, the Hunting Courtyard connects by means of four wings with other important areas of the Alcazar: the Lion's Courtyard –to the west–, the Palace of Peter I –to the east–, which was the main residence in the complex from the 14th century; the Crossing Courtyard –to the north–, which likewise connects with the Gothic Palace; and the Admiral's Quarters –to the south– headquarters to the *Casa de Contratación de Indias* from the 16th to 18th century.

Renovation. The poor condition of the paving led to its replacement in 1998. The new layout was inspired by former designs.

Fountain
On the far end of the courtyard is a small water fountain.

Access to the Crossing Courtyard

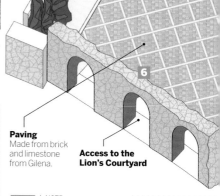

Paving
Made from brick and limestone from Gilena.

Access to the Lion's Courtyard

Almohad wall. The wall with three arches of the Muslim period still remains today despite successive projects to standardize the courtyard's façades.

> NOTE
> **HERALDIC ORNAMENTATION**

The central arch of the Almohad wall has remains of Mudejar decoration, with heraldry shields of Castile and León.

Mudejar. The façade of the Palace of Peter I.

Renaissance. Façade of the House of Trade.

Doorway to the Palace of Peter I

Upper palace
A grand staircase with ceramic tile skirting board leads into the apartment.

Admiral's Quarters
To the south of the courtyard was the former House of Trade for America.

1300
METRES SQUARE
is the approximate surface area of the Hunting Courtyard.

1998
IS THE YEAR
when work commences on the renovation of the paving.

2×2
METRES
is the measurement of the module of the square design of the courtyard paving.

The southern wing
Curiously, the most monumental element of the courtyard –the Palace of Peter I's façade– is on a level that is lower than the rest of the area. In the 16th century a Renaissance style project was approved of in order to give uniformity to the three remaining façades. Finally, only the south side was constructed –the façade of the House of Trade–, concluded in 1588 with 2 floors of canted brick arches, with Tuscan capitals lower down and Ionic ones higher up. In the second half of the 18th century the façade opposite was constructed in imitation.

Palace portico. The entrance of the royal residence of Peter I is presided by two marble fountains.

18th century. The north façade was constructed in 1755 using the same Renaissance resources as the south side –canted brick archways over marble columns with Tuscan and Ionic capitals–, this time without a gallery.

Admiral's Quarters

Under this designation are grouped together the rooms occupied since 1503 by the House of Trade for America.

Américo Vespucio
The Florentine navigator, to whom America owes its name, was senior navigator of the House of Trade.

16th and 17th centuries

The Admiral's Quarters is located to the south of the Hunting Courtyard, originally taken up by the *Alcázar Bendito* that the taifa king of Seville Al-Mutamid built in the 11th century. It actually comprises of three areas, result of the renovations carried out in the sector during the 16th and 17th centuries by the Catholic Monarchs and the House of Austria: the Admiral's Room and the Fan Room –rectangular– and the Chapel –squared–, on whose walls are paintings and objects from different eras.

Chapel

Admiral's Room

Fan Room

Lion's Courtyard

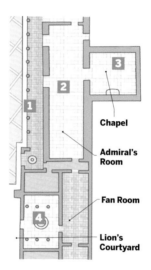

The Virgin of the Mariners
This is how sailors named her in the 16th century.

Arcaded gallery
The entrance to the Admiral's Quarters by means of the Hunting Courtyard is presided by the Renaissance gallery built in 1588.

NOTE
COLUMBUS AND THE HOUSE OF TRADE

Christopher Columbus made four journeys to America for the Crown of Castile between 1492 and 1504. After the second one, in 1496, Queen Isabella I received him in the Admiral's Quarters, where seven years later the *Casa de Contratación* was founded.

Admiral's Room

1503
IS THE YEAR in which the Catholic Monarchs create the *Casa de Contratación* in the Alcazar.

The coat of arms
The Chapel's walls are covered in tapestries with the coats of arms of the admirals of Castile such as Columbus.

LOCATION

Columbus
The explorer appears below the Virgin, to the left, in profile, with white beard.

Military quarters. Connects with the Lion's Courtyard.

90
METRES SQUARE is the surface area of the Chapel or Chapter House.

Saint Telmo
One of the sides of the altarpiece is dedicated to the Patron Saint of Sailors.

The Chapter House
Of squared ground plan, the Chapel or Chapter House is the room where navigators and geographers of the House of Trade for America held their meetings. Covered by a coffered ceiling from the 16th century, the room boasts an altarpiece of the *Virgin of the Mariners*, first work of art of religious character related to the discovery and conquest of America, an event that is clearly represented with the depiction of the different types of vessels from the Spanish fleet. The altarpiece was painted in 1535 by a Sevillian artist of German origin Alejo Fernández in a style of transition from the Gothic to the Renaissance.

Chapel or Chapter House

Detail of chapel ceiling

THE MODERN PATIOS. The rear sector of the Admiral's Quarters was renovated in the 18th century to be converted into the residence of the assistant chief magistrate, the representative of the king in the city. The zone, situated between the Prince's Garden and the Chapter House of the Admiral's Quarters, is divided into three patios. The Assistant one (1), of Castile style, has two levels, with Tuscan marble columns that support an upper wooden gallery; the Levies one (2), whose Mannerist arcades come from the house of the same name, located in the Jewish neighbourhood, Santa Cruz; and the Poets' Patio or the Joaquín Romero Murube Patio (3), a romantic and intimate space dedicated to the curator of the Alcazar between 1934 and 1969.

THE MUDEJAR ALCAZAR

The Palace of King Peter I

The Castilian Monarch valued the Muslim legacy and had the palace constructed according to the canons of Mudejar art.

The historical process of eight centuries traditionally called the Reconquest is usually summed up in history books as the Christians' fight to the death in order to recuperate control of the Iberian Peninsula, which the Muslims had occupied in almost all its entirety from the year 711. A less superficial study of this long period shows a very different reality. In the second half of the 14th century, Peter the Cruel I, King of Castile, not only admired Islamic culture and surrounded himself with Muslim advisors and Jews, but even signed a pact of mutual aid with the Nasrid Sultan of Granada –his theoretical enemy– in order to defend himself against his respective internal opponents. It is thanks to this open and conciliatory cultural and religious attitude that the walls of the Alcazar now house King Peter's palace. The Castilian monarch recognized the architectonic legacy of the Muslims and summoned artists and artisans of Arab and Bereber origin from Toledo, Granada and Seville in order to construct a new palace between 1364 and 1366 following the canons of Mudejar art, the style more genuinely Spanish, a combination of the cultures that intensely coexisted on the Peninsula for eight centuries despite being at heads on the battle field. It is a combination that allows for epigraphs on the palace walls such as "Glory to our Sultan Peter!", and "May Allah protect you!", a clear example of this cultural amalgamation. After its construction, the palace was converted into the usual residence of the Kings of Castile and later on of the Kings of Spain, and became the most splendid building of the ancient architecture of the Alcazar of Seville.

Peter I the Cruel
The Castilian monarch from the second half of the 14th century carried out the most decisive intervention in the history of the Alcazar: the construction of the palace.

A Muslim palace for the Christian king

Mudejar artists build the royal residence of Peter I

After spending part of his childhood and adolescence in the Alcazar, King Peter I decides to construct his new palace on the site of the former Muslim *Alcázar Bendito*, raised 300 years before, in order to convert it into his royal residence. The Castilian king had a Mudejar style building constructed that, in Muslim style, was structured around a large patio and had separate public and private areas.

A new ground plan

King Peter I decided to reorganize practically all the Alcazar complex situated to the south of the Gothic Palace and the Crossing Courtyard: he ordered the complete demolition of the ancient *Alcázar Bendito* of the 11th century and the construction, in its place, of a new royal residence with the façade overlooking a spacious courtyard –the Hunting one– whose dimensions were also defined during this period. The construction of the palace, completed in just two years was undertaken by Muslim artists and craftsmen.

The palace
Of square shape, has 2 façades –the east and the south one– that look on to the gardens, the west to the Hunting Courtyard, the north to the Gothic Palace.

1366

IS THE YEAR in which building work on the palace designed for Peter I is deemed finished. Construction had only taken 2 years.

The Infantes' Rooms
3 rooms transformed in the 19th century that face the Galley Garden.

Charles V Ceiling Room
Used as a chapel, it stands out for its ceiling (1543), one of the best in the history of Spanish art.

1

Access to Gothic Palace

Access to Upper Palace
The stair of the corridor between the vestibule and Maidens' Patio.

Royal chamber
Comprised of a regal chamber, a summer bedroom and a winter one.

The Maidens' Patio. The largest area of the palace backs up the rooms of the public zone. It has two levels: Mudejar style below and Renaissance style above.

Almohad vaults. Close up of the inside of the stair vaults, carried out in the Almohad period.

The vestibule. Constructed in such a way that no other room in the palace can be seen.

Hall of the Wasted Steps. It connects the Dolls' Patio with the Royal Chamber and the Maidens' Patio.

The Maidens' Patio. It is the nexus of connection of the private and residential area of the palace.

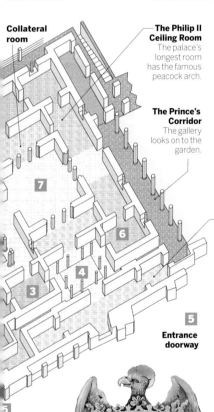

Collateral room

The Philip II Ceiling Room The palace's longest room has the famous peacock arch.

The Prince's Corridor The gallery looks on to the garden.

The Prince's Suite Also called the Queen's bedroom, it has three ceilings of different shapes.

Entrance doorway

3500
METRES SQUARE is the approximate surface area of the palace, including the patios of the Maidens and Dolls, and the Upper Palace.

Two patios for two uses

The palace is organized around two patios. The Maiden one, the largest, is surrounded by the rooms that are dedicated to the public life of the King, while the Dolls one, eight times smaller than the first, is the nucleus of the private area. Both functional centres intersect in the Ambassadors' Hall, a very monumental space in the palace and nexus of union between the two areas. This hall and the two patios are the only spaces that occupy the two floors of the palace, without interruptions.

The Ambassadors' Hall. Used by the kings as a Throne Room, where official receptions were celebrated, it is the most luxurious room of the Palace of Peter I.

The Room of the Catholic Monarchs The ceiling of the room is surrounded by heraldic emblems of the monarchs.

The main façade

Masterpiece of Mudejar art, the palace portico stands out from the other façades of the Hunting Courtyard.

The façade portico

The doorway in the centre of the façade, Mudejar work of 1364, is the paradigm of how the palace arrangement was built, given that in its construction many artisans of very different backgrounds collaborated. In the lower part, on a base of blocks of dressed stone that form a base of chiaroscuros, Sevillian artists carved blind polylobulated arches on both sides of the doorway and *sebqa* work higher up, directly inspired by the neighbouring Giralda tower. The lintel-like frame of the central door, in contrast, is work of Toledan masters, creators of the eleven voussoirs with *ataurique* work that makes up its original lintel. Between these voussoirs and the windows of the upper floor, a strip repeats polylobate blind arches on small columns.

The façade
With two levels, it has three parts: a central Mudejar one and two lateral ones from various later renovations.

Mullioned window
The centre of the façade has elegant columned windows.

Gallery
It was discovered in a restoration in the mid 20th century.

Roof of the Upper Palace

35
METRES
is the total width of Peter I's main façade, including the central module and the two lateral ones.

1370
IS THE YEAR
in which Muhammad V of Granada had the Comares' façade built in the Alhambra, inspired by the portico of the Palace of Peter I.

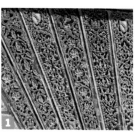

1 Doorway lintel. Ribbons of green tilework highlight the shapes of the voussoirs with *ataurique* work.

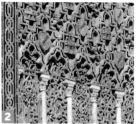

2 Central strip. Heraldic motifs (castles) and vegetables adorn the inside of the blind lobulated archways.

3 Upper gallery. Canted arches over marble columns on the upper level of the sides of the façade.

The symbolism on the walls
The plasterwork on the façade combines forms from nature with heraldic shields of King Peter I, of Castile and León.

LOCATION

Pinewood eaves

Brick pillars
They are on top of marble columns and frame the Mudejar portico.

Roof with Arabic tiles

Inscriptions

High up on the Mudejar portico, a large frieze reproduces inscriptions with Arabic characters in the centre –the motto of the Nasrid Dynasty of Granada is repeated up to eight times "and nobody is victorious, but Allah"– and Gothic calligraphy on the border, with details about the palace during the reign of Peter I. On the blind arches on the central strip, also in Arabic, is the phrase, "the empire for Allah", alternating with vegetable forms.

Upper eaves. Carpenters from Toledo carved a frieze of small arches decorated by wooden *muquarna* .

NOTE
MUDEJAR ART

Muslim art or a new style?
According to some historians, the Mudejar is no more than the permanence of Islamic art on the Peninsula after the disappearance of Muslim power. However, the adaptation of these forms to Christian customs generates a new and different style, which begins at the start of the 12th century and develops over the 4 centuries to follow.

The Maidens' Patio

A narrow passage from the vestibule leads to this patio, which palace activity revolved around.

'Plus ultra'
One of the mottos of the Catholic Monarchs appears on the patio's frieze, next to the heraldic coats of arms.

Centre of public life

Of rectangular form, the Maidens' Patio was the nucleus of the palace's official activity, with the Ambassadors' Hall –where the king received his subjects– on one far end and the chapel– today the Charles V Ceiling Room– on one of the sides. The arcaded patio's building, has two levels. The lower one, Mudejar style of the 14th century, has lobulated arches decorated with *sebqa* work, while the higher one, added in the 16th century, is made up of columns and Ionic capitals, and adorned with decorative plasterwork.

The location
Up against the northern wall of the Gothic Palace, the Maidens' Patio follows north-south orientation to the access façade to the Ambassadors' Hall.

640

METRES SQUARE
is the total surface area of the Maidens' Patio, including its four arcaded galleries.

The flower bed arches
The wall that covers the drop between the gallery floor and the garden is decorated with blind arches with a brick base, carried out in 1366.

 NOTE
THE PATIO OVER THE CENTURIES

Originally with just one floor and with the pond and the garden that can be admired today, the patio underwent many modifications in the 16th century: a 2nd level was added and it was paved.

1366

1572

1584

The faces
The gallery on the upper floor has medallions with the face of the emperor Charles V and the empress Isabella of Portugal.

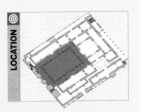

LOCATION

The patio's garden

Covered with marble paving for more than four centuries as a result of the renovation finished in 1572 during the reign of Philip II, the garden of the Maidens' Patio has (since the year 2002) a similar appearance to what it had after being constructed in Mudejar style in the fourteenth century. It is comprised of a longitudinal pond surrounded by brick paving and flower beds situated one metre below the gallery. As the latter wasn't designed to be used as a thoroughfare, the House of Austria decided to pave it.

Detail of Mudejar tiling

The Maidens' Patio

The decoration is a combination of the Mudejar work of the 14th century and Renaissance style of the 16th century.

1
Decoration
Close-up of stuccowork on the arches.

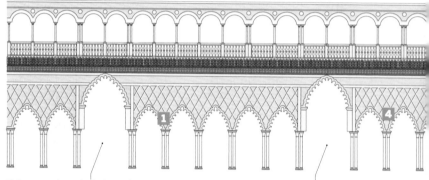

1 **4**

Entrance archway to Ambassadors' Hall

Entrance archway to the Royal Bedroom

Mudejar and Renaissance

The stuccowork on the patio's lower floor, carried out by Mudejar artisans between 1364 and 1366, reproduce works of *sebqa* of Almohad inspiration, while the interior walls of the gallery are also decorated in plasterwork, probably done by craftsmen from Granada. It is for this reason that in this space reappears the Nasrid motto "and nobody is victorious, but Allah" that can also be read on the façade. The decorative renovations carried out in the period of the House of Austria led to the addition of Renaissance style appearance plasterwork amongst the Mudejar work. Curiously enough, however, these additions do not alter the harmonious feel that the area transmits.

108
COLUMNS
are in the patio's galleries in groups of two and three: 52 Corinthians below and 56 Ionic ones above.

60
ARCHES
make up the patio's galleries. 24 lobulated ones on the lower gallery and 36 basket-handle arches.

1561
IS THE YEAR
when the substitution of some of the old columns of the lower gallery is carried out. Two years later the others are replaced.

The renovation
On the plaster on the inside of the courtyard the name of one of the artisans who worked on it and its construction date can be read.

LOCATION

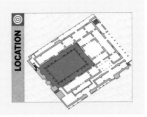

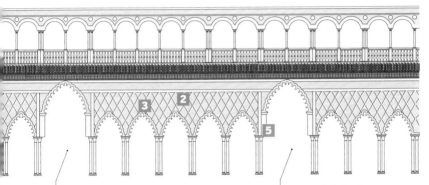

Archway in front of the Ambassadors' Hall

Entrance arch to the Charles V Ceiling Room

Plasterwork. During the 16th century the palace was adapted to the necessities of the imperial court. This meant that over the primitive Mudejar work silver Renaissance style elements were incorporated, and in the stuccowork equestrian and religious subjects, consoles with inscriptions and numerous heraldic coats of arms were to appear.

Ceilings of the galleries of the Maidens' Patio. Worked in polychrome wood, the ceilings of the four galleries of the patio boast decorative motifs based on *laceria* that interweaves to create geometric designs, stars with five, eight or ten points and diverse polygonal forms parting from a symmetric and repetitive organization of all the area. The inside of the mentioned polygons is painted with lively colours and some of them have incrusted decorative volumes with inscriptions, honeycomb work and heraldic coats of arms of Castile and León. These ceilings were put into place in the period of the Catholic Monarchs, at the end of the 15th century, and restored in 1856.

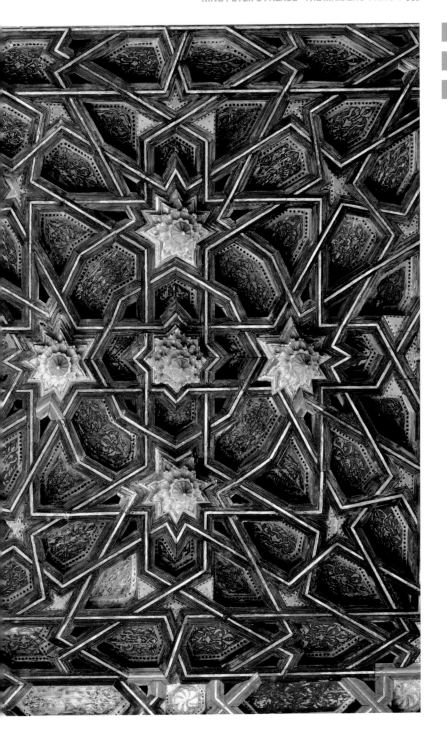

The tiles of the Maidens' Patio. The plinth courses of the galleries are decorated with tiles of geometric shapes. The tiling technique consists of positioning small ceramic pieces in a puzzle like way, face down, to form the motif. Once finished, it is covered with plaster and is applied on the wall. The composition principles respond to a systematic and symmetrical repetition of different simple geometric forms, such as stars and ribbons, until they achieve more complex combinations that form a uniform blanket.

The Infantes' Rooms

Overlooking the gardens, the palace's eastern wing originally consisted of a chapel and a room with two bedrooms.

Decoration on one of the doors

Three rooms

The Infantes' Rooms are three small rooms – a central rectangular one with a squared bedroom on each side – which look out on the Galley Garden by means of a balcony with stairway access. The side rooms respond to Muslim tradition, adopted by the Christian kings, by situating sleeping areas on both sides of a large room. Completely renovated during a refurbishment carried out in the mid 19th century, the lateral bedrooms as well as the central room, which was destined in some periods as dining room and in others as a simple storeroom, were used in principle as lodging for the Infantes, which was how these rooms obtained their name.

The palace's eastern wing
Made up of the Infantes' Rooms and the Charles V Ceiling Room, this area of the palace borders on its eastern side with the Galley Garden and Garden of Troy.

Charles V Ceiling Room
It was initially devised as palace chapel.

1848

IS THE YEAR
Marie Isabelle of Orléans, granddaughter of the last king of France, is born in the Infantes' central room.

1
Paving in the southern room

The Infantes' Rooms
They are made up of 3 areas.

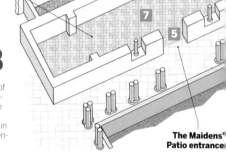
7
5

The Maidens' Patio entrance

2
Southern room of the Infantes

3
Access to Ambassadors' Hall

4
Window in one of the side rooms

The paving
The central room's floor, one of the few originals that remain in the palace, combines brick and tilework with heraldic images.

LOCATION

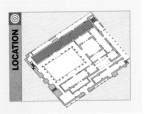

Exit to Galley Garden

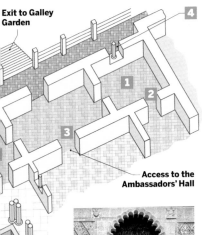

Access to the Ambassadors' Hall

Carpentry
The doorway to the Charles V Ceiling Room from the Maidens' Patio is a masterpiece by Toledan carpenters.

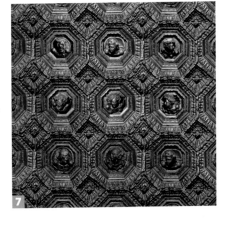

120
METRES SQUARE
is the approximate surface area of the three Infanta rooms.

100
METRES SQUARE
is the approximate area of the Charles V Ceiling Room.

<<<
Ceiling
The intricate and detailed coffered ceilings of the Infantes' Rooms are comprised of fine ribbons of wood of different colours alternating with heraldic coats of arms.

The Charles V Ceiling Room

Adjacent to the eastern gallery of the Maidens' Patio, the Charles V Ceiling Room was originally conceived to house the palace's chapel. The edification of the Oratory of the Catholic Monarchs allowed it to be renovated into a bedroom. It is at this time between 1541 and 1543, when the wooden coffered ceiling is installed, formed by octagonal and squared *casetones*, decorated with floral motifs and male and female busts. An arch with plasterwork divides the room into two areas: the smaller was used as the former chapel's presbytery and after the Renaissance style renovation it then became a bedroom.

The Royal Chamber

The original bedroom of the king in the palace, these two rooms open on to the western gallery of the Maidens' Patio.

Recycling
To redecorate the columns of the Royal Chamber, 10th century Cordovan capitals were used.

Winter and summer

Parallel to the western wall of the Maidens' Patio, whose gallery opens up by means of a large semi-circular arch, the Royal Chamber is a room that would have been used the king's bedroom and it is divided into two areas of rectangular ground plan. The first and widest is a royal chamber that receives light from the patio by means of two windows and includes, on one end, a squared bedroom separate from the salon by an arch from which hang curtains to ensure privacy and, on the opposite far end, a door connects with the private area of the palace. The second room, fresher and not as sunny, is the summer suite, which is accessed by crossing the three horseshoe arches.

Coat of arms. On the lower frieze are the emblems of Castile and León.

100
METRES SQUARE
is the surface area of the Royal Chamber, including the big and the small room.

Decoration
The walls are decorated with plasterwork with geometricized vegetable motifs combined with Arabic epigraphs.

LOCATION

3
Tile skirting board
The lower walls of the room are decorated with tiling of geometric design.

4
Entrance arch
Detail of vegetable motifs painted in the plasterwork.

5
Summer suite
Detail of ceiling carried out in polychrome plasterwork.

6
Skirting board ceramic piece

Luxurious decoration

Because of its probable function as monarch's bedroom, the decoration of the rooms is especially opulent. Many of the capitals that decorate the columns of these rooms originate from Cordovese palaces and were carved in the period of the Caliph (10th century), period of splendour for Muslim dominion on the Peninsula. The plasterwork is of Mudejar style (14th century) –amongst which stands out the fretwork of the three lattice windows located on the entrance archway to the room–, the tiled skirting boards with geometric motifs and the wooden doorway with two leaves, carved by Toledan cabinetmakers, while the ceiling of the royal chamber, based on geometric design lacework, is from the start of the 16th century.

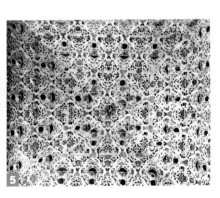

NOTE
DECORATION DETAIL

The horseshoe arches that connect the royal chamber with the summer suite display works with vegetable motifs amongst which a representation of shells particularly stands out, Muslim and Christian symbol linked to fertility and life.

The Ambassadors' Hall

Used as a Throne Room by Peter I and his heirs, the Ambassadors' Hall is the most opulent room in the palace.

Columns and capitals
The horseshoe archways are supported by Caliphal capitals and columns of pink and black marble.

Official receptions

Centre of the palace's public life where official receptions were held, the Ambassadors' Hall was the main room of the Alcazar. It has a squared ground plan and a semi-spherical wooden cupola –the image of Muslim *qubbas*– and it is open on its four sides: the main entrance, by means of a large canted archway, and the three others, by means of a triple horseshoe series of arches. The fact it is the only room that takes in the two levels of the palace –the outer roof of the cupola, hexagonal, is visible from the Maidens' Patio– is just more evidence of the Ambassadors' Hall's singularity.

The hall
Similar to the Cordovan palace of Medina Axahara, of the Caliph period (10th century), 3 of the 4 windows have triple horseshoe archways.

Star on cupola keystone
In the year 1843 some pieces of the cupola were substituted for mirrors in order to increase luminosity.

Philip II — Charles V

The gallery of kings. A frieze of paintings around the hall show the images of the kings of the Castilian territory from Recesvinto to Philip III.

Inscriptions
The plasterwork in the Hall makes up friezes with inscriptions in Arabic language and writing with praise to Allah and Peter I.

LOCATION

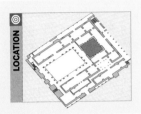

1526
IS THE YEAR
when the emperor Charles V and Isabella of Portugal celebrate their wedding in the Ambassadors' Hall.

The four balconies
Were made in tuned iron at the end of the 16th century.

The dragons
Each one of the four balconies in the Hall is supported by three dragons made from sheet metal.

The most sumptuous area
Peter I had the entire Hall decorated in order to convert it into the most luxurious room, with the walls totally covered in tiled skirting boards of Granadan inspiration and polychrome plasterwork with inscriptions full of praise to the king and Allah, and wooden doors with starred patterns and inscriptions around it. Half a century later, in 1427, the new wooden vault was installed.

NOTE
THE MAIN DOOR

Made in 1366, the two leaves of the door are surrounded by an Arabic inscription related to its construction, on the outside, and a Spanish inscription on the inside with biblical references,

Arabic inscription

01 and 04. Walls. Throughout the hall's perimeter there is delicate work in plaster decorated in golden and blue tones. **02. Castile and León.** In the central part of the cupola are coats of arms from Castile and León in reference to the origin of the King Peter I. **03. Portraits.** Painted in the cupola's wooden frieze, there are 32 and probably reproduce the faces of the Princesses and Infantes. *Following page.* **The cupola.** Carved in wood, in the restoration of 1843, mirrors were added to provide more luminosity.

The collateral rooms

These two symmetrical rooms connect the Ambassadors' Hall with the private areas of the palace.

1598
IS THE YEAR in which the wooden ceilings were finished based on coffere based on coffere ceilings of geometric design.

Ceilings and plasterwork

The collateral rooms are two rectangular spaces that flank the Ambassadors' Hall and connect it to the Dolls' Patio –centre of the private sector of the palace– and the Infantes' Rooms. They are characterized by their ceilings, which date from the last years of the reign of Philip II, at the end of the 16th century, and by their original Mudejar plasterwork friezes with horse-riding scenes with white silhouettes. Those on the eastern side, inspired by a contemporary book called *Crónica troyana*, (Troy Chronicle), were carried out by Toledo masters, while later ones in the opposite room are by Sevillian artists.

East room. Paving, walls and ceiling of the eastern room, with the Ambassadors' Hall to the left.

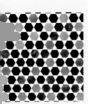

The tilework
As in the rest of the palace, the collateral rooms have a tiled skirting board shaped, in this case, with pieces of hexagonal and triangular form.

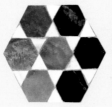

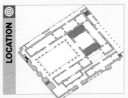

Plasterwork medallions
Mudejar artists from Toledo worked with plaster material to represent silhouettes of horses, women, real and fantastical animals, trees and plants.

27

MEDALLIONS
of plasterwork with horse-riding scenes are located on the upper frieze of each one of the collateral rooms.

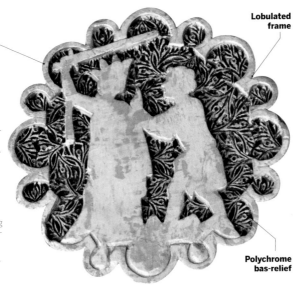

Lobulated frame

Polychrome bas-relief

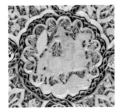

NOTE
TRANSITION FROM THE PRIVATE TO PUBLIC AREA

The collateral rooms serve as transition areas between the private and public zones of the palace and are useful in the respect that they adapt the Ambassadors' Hall arrangement to the width of the Maidens' Patio.

Ambassadors' Hall

1 | 2

1. East room
2. West room

Access
Connection with the Maidens' Patio.

The Philip II Ceiling Room

The largest room in the palace is distinguished by its triple archway entrance and its semi-barrelled vault.

Peacock archway
Decorative detail

The peacock arch

The arches that connect the Philip II Ceiling Room with the Ambassadors' Hall is one of the most beautiful examples of Mudejar decoration in the entire palace. Formed by three horseshoe arches, inspired by the architecture of 10th century Cordova and supported by two marble black columns with caliphal capitals, this archway combines in its decoration various Muslim resources –stylized plant motifs, Arabic inscriptions in *Cufic* calligraphy and works of *laceria*– with Christian motifs: figurative plant motifs and, above all, the different birds that give the archway its name and show the interest that King Peter I had for hunting and, in particular, for falconry.

The birds
Likened to similar works in plaster in the Mudejar palace of Tordesillas, in Valladolid, built by Alfonso XI and Peter I.

24

BIRDS
of many different species, including two peacocks are represented on the archway.

23

METRES
is the total length of the Philip II Ceiling Room, the longest room in Peter I's palace.

Peacock
The name of the arch.

Shell

Inspiration
The silhouettes of birds are inspired by motifs adorning the fabrics that arrived in Seville from markets from the Orient.

Swan
Symbol of beauty and elegance.

South-facing. The light of midday illuminates the plasterwork on the peacock arch by means of a doorway and two windows that look out on to the Prince's Garden.

Natural motifs
The decoration of the room, based on vine tendrils and other natural forms, it is of Mudejar style from the 14th century.

LOCATION

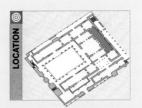

Horseshoe arch

The ceiling. Carpenter Martín Infante was inspired by Italian Sebastiano Serlio, whose treatment of architecture was highly acclaimed in the sixteenth century.

Inspiration
Constructed in the 14th century, the arch reproduces the architectonic forms of the Palace of Medina Azahara, near Cordova.

Epigraphs
The arch combines natural motifs, figurative images and ornamental Arabic inscriptions.

The semi-barrelled vault

The two names by which the room between the Ambassadors' Hall and the gallery overlooking the Prince's Garden is known by refer to its ceiling. For the lightly arched curve that the wooden ceiling adopts, it receives the name of the Room of the Semi-barrelled Vault; for the time of its construction, it is called the Philip II Ceiling Room as it is a masterpiece of Mannerist carpentry work carried out between 1589 and 1591 – in the latter part of the reign of the Second of the Austrias– based on boxes whose interior squared reliefs alternate with crossed reliefs.

The Dolls' Patio

Eight times smaller than the Maidens' Patio, this Mudejar jewel is the backbone of the palace's private zone.

Capitals
One of the capitals of the arch that houses the dolls, is of the Caliphal era and has inscriptions from the Koran sculpted.

In search of privacy

Designed to preserve the privacy of the residential sector, the Dolls' Patio connects with the vestibule by means of a narrow bent corridor that avoids indiscreet looks. It also opens on to three bedrooms, to one of the collateral rooms and to the Prince's Garden via an independent passage. Originally of just one floor, a Mannerist style gallery was added on in the 16th century and then disappeared in the 19th century when the mezzanine, the historicist gallery and the skylight were built.

Tiled paving
The sobriety of the marble floor, with a small step between the patio and portico, contrasts with the richness of the tiles, work of artisans from Granada.

80 METRES SQUARE
is the patio, including its arcaded arrangement.

Plasterwork
The originals (photos) are on the ground floor. The upper floor ones were attached to the wall in the C19th from moulds extracted from the Alhambra.

 NOTE
THE PATIO'S DOLLS

The name of the patio is due to four tiny heads that are sculpted at the start of the arch nearest to the corridor that leads to the vestibule of the palace entrance. The small plaster sculptures appear in relief and are inscribed in a circle.

10

COLUMNS
of Caliphal style
(10th century),
ecycled by Al-
Mutamid, sup-
port the gallery's
0 arches.

Gallery ceilings
They are made
up of wooden
panelled ceilings
with geometric
polychrome *laceria* motifs of lively
colour.

LOCATION

Artists from Granada

For the dynamic asymmetry of its two smaller sides, for its cosy and intimate dimensions and for its delicate decoration, the Dolls' Patio is one of the jewels of the Al-cazar. The white, black and pink marble columns with caliphal capitals – rescued from the Cordovan palace of Medina Azahara in the 11th century by king Al-Muta-mid– support canted semi-circular arches that are greatly influenced by the Nasrid art in this construction. The Dolls' Patio is, in effect, work of artists sent by the Granada Sultan Mu-hammed V, friend and ally of Peter I. These Mudejar plasterers show their skill in the work of the *atauriques* (stylized plant motifs) technique, the wall sections, the arches and the upper frieze of lobulated arches that decorate the ground floor.

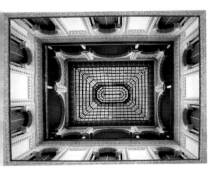

Upper floors
They were constructed in the mid 19th century by architect Rafael Contreras, responsible also for the restoration of the Alhambra.

Window
Arch on mezzanine of the Dolls' Patio.

The Catholic Monarchs' Room

This room, parallel to the Dolls' Patio, is known for its sixteenth century Renaissance coffered wooden panelled ceiling.

1

Renaissance ceiling

The Room of the Catholic Monarchs' Ceiling is one of the two squared rooms that look out on to the smaller sides of the Dolls' Patio. It also leads into the Philip II Ceiling Room and has a 19th century window, overlooking the Prince's Garden. The plasterwork that goes around the entrances is Mudejar while the *lazo* ceiling, comprised of wooden ribbons of different colours and surrounded by heraldic emblems of the Catholic Monarchs, is a Renaissance work following the Siege of Granada (1492).

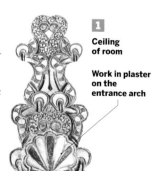

1

Ceiling
of room

Work in plaster
on the
entrance arch

Arrocabe
The frieze that goes around the ceiling has candelabra motifs and pomegranates, in memory of the recently sieged city.

Inscriptions
The polychrome plasterwork on the 14th century Mudejar door frames and entrances include Arabic inscriptions.

LOCATION

12

WOOD COATS OF ARMS
are on the frieze going around the ceiling.

 2

Granada
The Catholic Monarchs' shield incorporates the Nasrid pomegranate emblem.

 3

The arrows
They symbolize the reign of Ferdinand of Castile by coinciding with his initial.

 4

The yoke
Shield with Isabella's initial, and the motto "They amount to the same".

 5

Room entrances

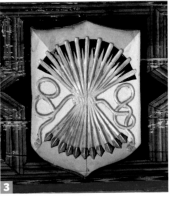

NOTE
THE PAVING IN THE ROOM

This room is one of the few remaining rooms with original paving, a combination of brickwork and tile pieces –called *olambrillas*– framed by a border of glazed ceramic work.

The Prince's Suite

The queen's former bedroom is divided into three rooms with priceless Renaissance ceilings.

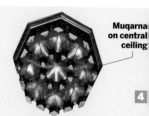

Muqarna on central ceiling

4

The queen's former bedroom

With direct access from the Dolls' Patio, the Prince's Suite was the Queen's bedroom until Isabella I of Castile (*Isabel la Católica*) had new rooms built in the Upper Palace. Its configuration follows Muslim tradition, with a long central room and a squared bedroom on with either side, delimited by arches. The southern room, leading to the Prince's Garden and with a staircase to the Upper Palace, has one of the best Renaissance style ceilings on the Peninsula, based on polychrome wooden panelling.

The successor's bedroom
Juan de Trastámara was born in the Alcazar in 1478 and occupied this bedroom during his stays in Seville.

1

The Prince's Suite

2

Access to the Dolls' Patio

3

Bedrooms

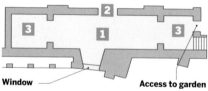

Window

Access to garden

NOTE
THE WINDOW TO THE HUNTING COURTYARD

The central room of the Prince's Suite incorporates a window to the gallery of the Admiral's Quarters, on the Hunting Courtyard. This opening, subsequent to the Catholic Kings, was carried out to provide more natural light to these bedrooms.

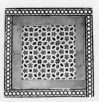

The room's floors
Designed at the end of the 20th century, the paving combines the use of brick and ceramic tile work.

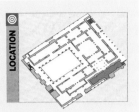

LOCATION

19
YEARS OLD
is the age that Prince Juan de Trastámara died of tuberculosis, the last hope for the Catholic Monarchs to have a direct successor.

5

Central ceiling
Polychrome ribbonwork generates 12-pointed stars with heraldic images that are combined with muqarna work.

6

South ceiling
Done in 1543, it is is made up of polychrome panneled work with interlacing, muqarna and plateresque mouldings.

7

Plasterwork
Polychrome plasterwork on the triangles of the arches.

FOLLOWING PAGE
Ceiling of the north room
Renaissance wooden panelled ceiling with muqarna and a frieze with heraldic motifs.

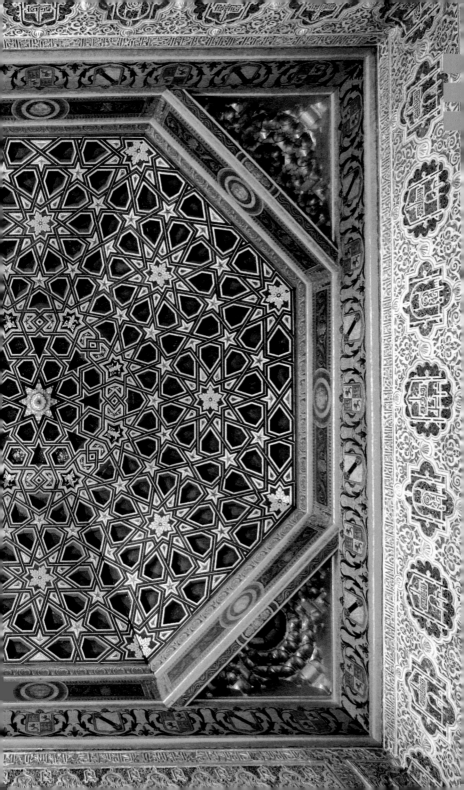

The Upper Palace

The monarchs' winter residence in the Alcazar

Although some rooms on the upper floor already existed when Mudejar artisans finished building the Palace of Peter I in 1366, the enlargement of this level was commissioned by the Catholic Monarchs, towards the end of the 15th century and start of the 16th, and completed during the reign of the first Austrias, to duplicate the distribution of the original palace, on the floor above for its residential use in the winter.

Two palaces in one

Until the intervention of the Catholic Monarchs, the upper floor only had two rooms: the Assembly Hall, to the west of the palace, and the bedroom of King Peter I, on the eastern corner. The rest of the palace only took up one floor. Despite the good climate, with mild nights during most of the year, the Catholic Monarchs believed it convenient to build on the upper floor, protected from the cold and damp of the ground, in order to make the winter months much more tolerable and comfortable.

Royal abode
The Upper Palace is a residence for Kings on their visits to Seville. Its rooms hold a large collection of furniture, most dating back to the 19th century.

1300
METRES SQUARE
is the approximate surface area of the Upper Palace, except for the courtyards and Ambassadors' Hall.

Upper gallery of the Maidens' Patio
Built in the C16th in Renaissance style.

The Catholic Monarchs viewpoint

Bedroom of King Peter I

Hercules Room
So-called, in the C16th, the collection of rooms in this area of the Upper Palace.

Access to the Upper Palace. The stairs, from the end of the 16th century, at the far end of the gallery of the Admiral's Quarters, allow access from the Hunting Courtyard.

Hercules columns. On the outside of the cupola of the Ambassadors' Hall is this Catholic Monarch's symbol.

Main façade

Assembly Hall
Its walls are decorated with Mudejar polychrome plasterwork.

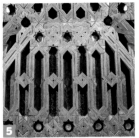

The Queen's Antechamber
Original ceiling, carried out in the period of the Catholic Monarchs.

Catholic Monarchs' viewpoint
The characteristic twinned horseshoe arches, from the Garden of Troy.

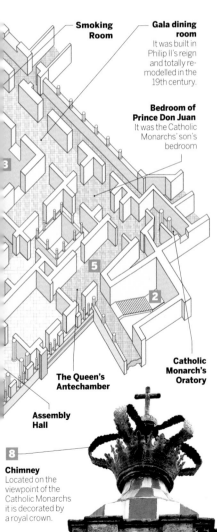

Smoking Room

Gala dining room
It was built in Philip II's reign and totally remodelled in the 19th century.

Bedroom of Prince Don Juan
It was the Catholic Monarchs' son's bedroom

The Queen's Antechamber

Assembly Hall

8

Chimney
Located on the viewpoint of the Catholic Monarchs it is decorated by a royal crown.

Catholic Monarch's Oratory

1591
IS THE YEAR when the Smoking Room's ceiling is carved, attributed to a master carpenter named Martín Infante.

Access stairs
Detail of the ceiling of the stair from the Hunting Courtyard.

Residential function

The extension sponsored by the Catholic Monarchs and the complete renovations introduced a few decades later by the first Austrias led to an Upper Palace with a layout that was almost identical to that on the ground floor: the galleries going around the patios of the Maidens and Dolls were used to connect different areas. In this case, however, residential activity took up more of the palace area than public activity, which was confined to the Assembly Hall and its collateral rooms.

Bedroom of King Peter. Detail of the skirting board with geometric ribboned motifs that decorates this room situated on the eastern corner of the Upper Palace.

The oratory

Despite its small area, the oratory is considered to be the city of Seville's finest Renaissance masterpiece.

The Queen's Suite
The oratory is found in the rooms of the Queen's Suite, the bedrooms that Isabella I of Castile had built in the Upper Palace.

The oratory

Located on the western corner of the Upper Palace, the oratory of the Catholic Monarchs is a little room, rectangular, covered by ribbed crossed vaults and supported by two columns that generate four basket-handle arches adorned with flamboyant filigree work. The altar is presided over by an altarpiece of tiles made by the Tuscan artist Francesco Niculoso Pisano, great innovator of 16th century ceramic work that fused Andalusian tradition with Italian decorative technique.

The Visitation
The central theme of Niculoso Pisano's altarpiece in the oratory relates the *Visitation of the Virgin to Elizabeth* scene.

1504
IS THE YEAR
in which Niculoso completed the oratory altarpiece, coinciding with Isabella I of Castile's death.

The Monarchs' viewpoint
Detail of Mudejar ribbon work below a window.

Assembly Hall

NOTE
THE UPPER PALACE CEILINGS

Despite the fact that they have been transformed over the centuries and up to now for use by royal residents, most of the Upper Palace's rooms retain the original panelled ceilings of the 15th and 16th centuries.

Tile of cultural fusion
Niculoso Pisano uses tiles like canvas, in contrast to the typical geometric shapes of Muslim tilework.

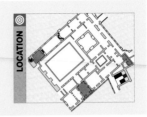

LOCATION

More ancient rooms

Single Mudejar rooms of the Upper Palace, the Assembly Hall and the bedroom of King Peter are the most sumptuous of the floor. The walls of the Assembly Hall appear completely decorated with tiled skirting boards and plasterwork on the rest of the walls. Its outer side opens out on to a muqarna covered gallery with views of the Hunting Courtyard, the Giralda and the cathedral. King Peter's bedroom, on the opposite end of the palace, conserves Mudejar wooden panelling dating from the start of the 15th century and Mudejar skirting boards with ribbon work.

THE FIRST CHRISTIAN WORK IN THE ALCAZAR

The Gothic Palace and the Crossing Courtyard

Alfonso X the Wise had his royal residence built within the Alcazar in the Western Medieval Christian style.

Ferdinand III, the King of Castile that conquered Seville in 1248, hardly had enough time to enjoy the Alcazar, given that he died there four years later. Alfonso X the Wise, his successor, inherited his father's admiration for Islamic art and his predilection for Seville. However, the palace that the Almohad Caliphs had inhabited did not adapt to the lifestyle of the Castilian king nor to the necessities of his court. In contrast to Muslim taste for the proliferation of relatively reduced spaces of moderate height, with labyrinth-like distributions designed to maintain privacy, the Christian monarchs opposed these preferences and opted for lofty and spacious rooms, and for clear hierarchy in the different areas of the palace. It is for this reason, and for the prestige that Gothic art, imported from France a few decades before, had acquired on the Peninsula, Alfonso X chose this style to construct his palace inside the Alcazar. The Gothic forms, moreover, were by then fully identified with Christianity and the Crusades. His choice, for it, symbolized the victory of the Christian Western world over Islam. With that intention, the King of Castile invited masons who had constructed the naves of Burgos Cathedral, one of the high points of the Gothic style on the Peninsula, in order to build his royal residence on the remains of the former Almohad palace and set up his court there of legislators and intellectuals that would return the Alcazar the splendour it had displayed in the era of Al-Mutamid, the poet king of the taifa of Seville.

Alfonso X the Wise
King of Castile between 1252 and 1284, he composed his famous (*Cantigas de Santa María*), written in Gaelic-Portuguese, in his Gothic Palace of the Alcazar.

Gothic Palace and Crossing Courtyard

The first work by the Christian kings in the Alcazar

Erected by Alfonso X from 1254, more than a century before Peter I's palace, the Gothic Palace was planned with the help of Castilian masons expert in French Gothic forms after years of work on the Cathedral of Burgos. The first Christian intervention in the Alcazar was raised on the remains of the Almohad palace, next to the Crossing Courtyard that provides the backbone of this area of Muslim origin.

The Gothic Palace

Situated to the east of the Hunting Courtyard, between the Crossing Courtyard and the gardens of the Alcazar, the Gothic Palace is comprised of four rooms: two parallel larger ones, presided by a portico that acts as courtyard gallery, and two smaller ones, which are located on the far ends of the formers. Originally, all these rooms were covered with ribbed cross vaults of typical Gothic style. Outside, the crenellated buttresses and the small angular towers also give away their constructor's desire to introduce Western world Christian forms into the very heart of the Alcazar palace.

1500
METRES SQUARE

is the approximate surface area of the Gothic Palace, including the portico.

1252
IS THE YEAR

in which Alfonso X, responsible for the Gothic Palace, is crowned King of Castile and León on his father's death, Ferdinand III, conqueror of Seville in 1248.

The courtyard and palace
The arcaded galleries built in the C18th after the Lisbon earthquake, back the Crossing Courtyard with the Gothic Palace, to the east, and with the Hunting Courtyard to the west.

Castile and León
It's shield is over the Gothic Palace's entrance.

Lanterns of the María Padilla Baths

Gothic palace portico
Designed by the Flemish or Dutch engineer Sebastián van der Borcht in the C18th, he follows the Baroque line of the Crossing Courtyard.

Entrance portico to the Mounting Block and the Hunting Courtyard

Portico. The palace is accessed by the courtyard gallery.

The Vault Room. The Gothic structure is from the C13th.

Entrance to the María Padilla Baths
A tunnel crosses the foundations of the Gothic Palace.

Access to the Chapel

Sculpture on the portico
Detail of the entranceway to the Gothic Palace.

4

Lantern of the Tapestry Room
Located on the terraced roof that was used as palace parade ground, it is from the 18th century and provides the room with light.

3

4

5

2

The Chapel
Just like the Earthenware Room, symmetrical to this, it is covered with Gothic vaults and its walls decorated with tiled skirting boards.

Flowerbed

The Crossing Courtyard

Basic enclave of the Muslim palace, the Crossing Courtyard has survived as a space of communication in the Alcazar despite having undergone many modifications throughout its eight centuries of existence. Its almost squared dimensions, framed by 4 sides –two of them are arcaded–, maintain the original appearance of a cross by means of 2 paved thoroughfares that cross over each-other forming 4 flowerbeds.

Iron cross

Vane

4

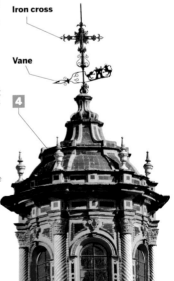

1760

IS THE YEAR
renovation of the Crossing Courtyard and Gothic Palace was complete after the 1755 earthquake.

The Tapestry Room
The first room of the Gothic Palace was totally reconstructed in Baroque style after having been seriously affected by the earthquake of 1755.

The Crossing Courtyard

Its present sober appearance makes it hard to imagine the ingenious configuration that astonished the king's guests.

The endings
The Gothic Palace's original façade was extremely sober. The 18th century renovation brought these cup shapes.

Two levels

Built by the Almohads towards the end of the 12th century, the original Crossing Courtyard had two levels. The upper one was made up of two walkways that crossed over and four others that went around the rectangular perimeter. The lower one, composed of vaulted galleries which supported the mentioned walkways. A pool took up the centre of the longest gallery and around it were gardens with aromatic plants and fruit trees, whose tops reached the height of people strolling along the walkways. The 1755 earthquake seriously affected the structure, and it was decided to fill in the courtyard to the height of the upper level, which is how it appears now.

The courtyard portico
In the west wing, built in Baroque style in the latter half of the 18th century, with lintel-like portal and pediment split by a balcony.

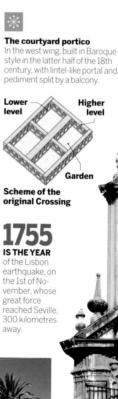

Lower level / **Higher level**

Garden

Scheme of the original Crossing

1755
IS THE YEAR of the Lisbon earthquake, on the 1st of November, whose great force reached Seville, 300 kilometres away.

Circular pediment
The ending of the intermediate section contrasts with the straight and triangular pediments on the lower floor and loft.

The paving. The thoroughfares of the Crossing Courtyard are comprised of paving stones positioned on their side in diagonal, generating a wheat ear design.

4 GARDENS
one in each corner, have always been present in all the different layouts of the courtyard.

The Alcazar archive
The rooms in the north wing of the Crossing Courtyard hold the documental background of the Royal Alcazar.

LOCATION

950
METRES SQUARE
is the area of the Crossing Courtyard, without counting galleries or the María Padilla Baths.

1

The baths
Ten small cross vaults cover the pool that goes through the subterranean gallery.

2

The grotto
In 1578 a fountain-grotto of naturalist style was constructed on the western end of the baths.

3

Ventilation and illumination
Openings in the floor give light and air to the Baths.

The María Padilla Baths

The roof on the lower level of the Crossing Courtyard, built after the earthquake of 1755, created an underground gallery formed by the former pool and the Gothic cross vaults which Alfonso X had made to reinforce the old Almohad structure towards the end of the 13th century. This gallery, known as the María Padilla Baths because it was the favourite corner of Peter I's lover, is reached by means of a tunnel with an entrance in the Dance Garden that passes close to the foundations of the Gothic Palace.

NOTE
THE AUSTERE COURTYARD

In contrast to the almost theatrical drama of the Sevillian Baroque, Sebastián van der Borcht's projects in the Crossing Courtyard and the Gothic Palace stand out for their restraint and sobriety.

The Vault Room

Charles V and Isabella of Portugal's wedding in 1526 influenced this room whose tiles pay homage to the emperor.

2
Corbels
In the C16th refurbishment the engaged columns were substituted

Gothic ceilings

The wing of the Gothic Palace opening on to the gardens of the Alcazar is occupied by the Vault Room, so-called because it conserves the Gothic cross vaults erected during the reign of Alfonso X the Wise. Originally, the vaults in this room —one metre narrower than the parallel Tapestry Room— rested on columns joined to the walls. However, the complete refurbishment of the Gothic Palace carried out during the reign of Philip II, between 1577 and 1583, eliminated these pillars and converted them into corbels so that the walls of the room could hold the Mannerist tilework that decorates all the skirting board. These tiles of great artistic value as well as the attractive windows that absorb the light from the gardens, open in the same period, break with the original austerity of the Gothic work.

The room
Very long, it connects with the gardens, Chapel and the Earthenware Room on its far ends, and with the Tapestry Room in the centre.

300
METRES SQUARE
is the approximate surface area of the Vault Room, including the corridor to the garden.

1

Lamp
Four pieces light the room.

NOTE
GOTHIC PALACE ROYAL WEDDING

The rooms of the Gothic Palace were called the Rooms of Charles V due to the wedding banquet of the emperor and Isabella of Portugal, celebrated in the Vault Room the 11th of March of 1526.

1577
IS THE YEAR
when repair work commenced along with the remodelling of the Gothic Palace, built during the reign of Alfonso X the Wise, 300 years before.

3

Mannerism. Corbel in the Vault Room.

4

The paving tiles
The laurel crowns drawn on four pieces of ceramic work are combined with white marble pieces.

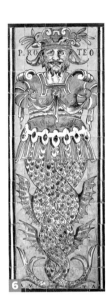

5 **6**

Allegorical figures
Separating the different panels of tiles, mythological beings and allegorical figures represent *thought* (5), *imagination*, Proteus (6) –Greek god of the sea and Metra, the daughter of Greek God Eresictón.

7

Corridor to the Pond Garden
It was remodelled and enlarged between 1576 and 1577.

The tiles

Manufactured between 1577 and 1578 by the potter of Sicilian origin called Cristóbal de Augusta, the tiled skirting boards of the Vault Room pay tribute to Charles V –dead twenty years before– and his wife Isabella of Portugal. With a predominant yellow background and use of blue, white, green and ochre tones for the figures, the tiles are organized as if they were tapestries, with panels of naturalist motifs and busts of the emperor and empress, surrounded by friezes and columns with faunal, heraldic and legendary themes.

Tapestry Room and Chapel

With the refurbishment in the 18th century, the Tapestry Room lost the Gothic identity that the Chapel still conserves.

The Tapestry Room

Similar until 1755 to the parallel Vault Room –with Gothic cross vault ceiling and Renaissance tiled skirting boards–, the Tapestry Room was totally overhauled after the Lisbon earthquake in a late Baroque style, using a transverse arch and pendentive domes instead of the original cross vaults. With the aim to improve lighting in the room, in the same period a central lantern was built that juts out from the upper terrace of the palace until it becomes visible from the Crossing Courtyard. The walls of the room are decorated with tapestries woven by Flemish artists in the 18th century according to 16th century originals of the same origin and dedicated to the military exploits of Charles V.

The room
Van der Borcht used pendentive domes supported by transverse arches on corbels.

The lamp
t hangs from the lantern that lights the room.

1982
IS THE YEAR
in which the constitution of the first Andalusian Parliament in history was held in the Tapestry Room of the Royal Alcazar of Seville.

The tapestries. Woven in Madrid's Royal Factory of Tapestry and commissioned by Philip V, they reproduce Charles V's victorious campaign against Tunisia.

1

Castile and León
The pendentive domes in the Tapestry Room are decorated with royal coats of arms.

The angels of the chapel
11 of these small images decorate the moulding of the arch that goes around the Virgin of Antigua altarpiece.

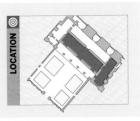

LOCATION

2

3

The altarpiece
The 18th century carving holds an anonymous C17th copy of the Virgin of Antigua.

Tiles
Detail of Chapel skirting board.

1577

IS THE YEAR
Asensio de Maeda introduces the corbels and skirting boards in the chapel.

The Chapel

On the far south end of the Gothic Palace, the Chapel –dedicated by Alfonso X to Saint Clemente in 1271– conserves the cross vault Gothic ceilings and, like the Vault Room, was refurbished towards the end of the 16th century, losing engaged columns in favour of Mannerist corbels so that tile skirting boards from the same creator could be installed with similar theme to those in the parallel room, though this time without heraldic motifs. The chapel is presided over by an 18th century altarpiece with the Virgin of Antigua, a copy of a painting from Seville Cathedral.

03

The Royal Alcazar gardens

The artistic evolution of the Muslim orchards

With a surface area that quadruples the different constructions that make up the Alcazar, the gardens stretch to the south and east of the palace, a zone of orchards and open land that has mostly stayed within the walls the Almohads raised in the 12th century. Today, after a millennium of natural and artistic evolution, they make up one of the most important arrangements of European gardening.

For the five senses

The origin of the gardens of the Alcazar is found in the The Alcove Orchard (*Huerta de la Alcoba*), which the Muslims cultivated to the east of the palace. Originally from very arid lands, they took every care to transform the plots into a pleasure for the senses; they grew a wide variety of fruit trees, flowers of all variety of shapes, colours and textures, they sowed aromatic plants and perfumed flowers, used the pond water as a mirror and the fountains to create relaxing sounds, and they opened windows and viewpoints in their palaces in order to have the best outlook. In fact, the Koran, Islam's sacred book, likens paradise to a garden.

Garden-plot
Varieties from the Orient were cultivated, like date palm trees, the pomegranate, the pepper or saffron.

1
Marquis' Garden of Retreat

2
The Poets' Garden

3
English Garden

4
The Damsels' Garden

5
The Alcove Garden

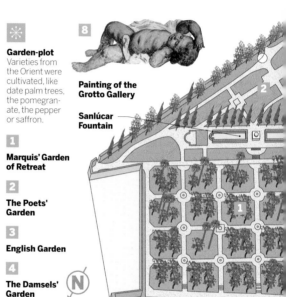

8

Painting of the Grotto Gallery

Sanlúcar Fountain

(N)

Wall-aqueduct
The Alcazar's water supply passed inside this section of the wall.

The Marchena – Gateway

NOTE
MARCHENA GATEWAY

Heraldic motifs
The gateway of the palace of the Dukes of Arcos (A), was moved to the Alcazar from the town of Marchena in 1913, a Gothic work from the end of the 15th century that stands out for heraldic motifs -the eagle (B) and the lion (C) that crown its structure.

A
B
C

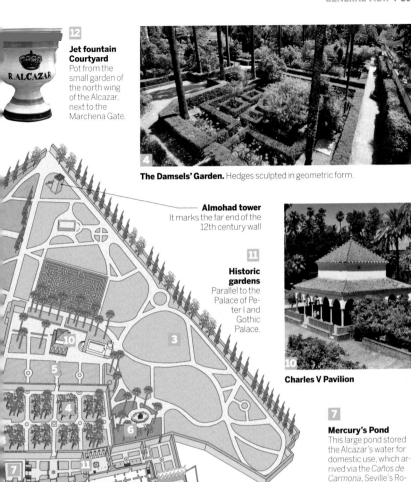

12
Jet fountain Courtyard
Pot from the small garden of the north wing of the Alcazar, next to the Marchena Gate.

The Damsels' Garden. Hedges sculpted in geometric form.

Almohad tower
It marks the far end of the 12th century wall

11
Historic gardens
Parallel to the Palace of Peter I and Gothic Palace.

Charles V Pavilion

7
Mercury's Pond
This large pond stored the Alcazar's water for domestic use, which arrived via the *Caños de Carmona*, Seville's Roman aqueduct.

Artistic trends

Since the Christian conquest, the Muslim gardens turned into gardens that show the evolution of art by combining nature and architecture, from the unmistakable mark of the Mannerist style that Italian Vermondo Resta left in the areas nearest to the palace at the start of the 17th century, including romantic naturalism, historicism and English landscaping, also represented in the Alcazar.

6
The Cross Garden
It held the old maze, disappeared in 1910.

9
The Alcubilla Patio
Behind the modern archways of one of the galleries of this patio a series of original Mudejar style arches are conserved.

Philip V arms
Ceramic coat of arms in the Alcubilla Patio.

The historic gardens

The section adjacent to the Palace of Peter I and Gothic Palace is occupied by the Alcazar's oldest gardens.

Castle
The arch that connects the Gardens of T... and Flower G... den is presid... by the Castili... crown done i... plaster.

Fragmentation

The so-called historic gardens occupy a strip on the corner that goes round the east and south façades of the Palaces of Peter I and Alfonso X. This sector forms the original nucleus of the gardens of the Alcazar and it is made up of six different areas with hardly any botanic or architectonic relationship, despite the fact that all have their origin under Muslim dominion –a time from which they have inherited this Andalusian tendency to compartmentalization– and were definitively planned by architect Vermondo Resta at the start of the 17th century, during Philip III's reign. This Mannerist refurbishment went more deeply into fragmentation and gave the arrangement a series of mythological themes that have remained translated to their modern name.

NOTE
THE GALLEY GARDEN

Homage to poet King Al-Mutamid
The Galley Garden has a marble column dedicated to the 11th century poet-king, whose death in his exile to Morocco prevented him from being able to enjoy his dear *Alcázar Bendito*.

1

The Prince's Garden
A Renaissance C16th gallery connects it with the rooms of Peter I's Palace.

2

The Flower Garden
It holds a Mannerist grotto-fountain from the C17th with a Charles V bust.

3

The Galley Garden
It used to hold the structure of a wooden boat that squirted streams of water.

4

Garden of Troy
Its central fountain is decorated with pipes with lion heads of Muslim manufacture dating from the C10th.

5

The Dance Garden
In this space can be found the entrance to the tunnel that leads to the María Padilla Baths, below the Crossing Courtyard.

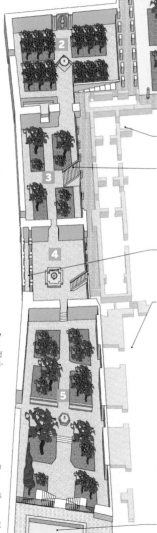

Palace of Peter I

Access to the Infante Rooms
By means of a pergola supported by Renaissance pedestals.

Rustic gallery
It combines plaster with carved stone.

Gothic Palace

3400
METRES SQUARE
is the approximate surface area of the six historic gardens.

1570
IS THE YEAR
in which work starts on the Alcove Orchard to transform it into various gardens.

The Pond Garden

6

GARDENS

of small dimension make up the arrangement of historic gardens of the Alcazar of Seville.

The Flower Garden
The small pond found in this garden is decorated with flat ceramic tiles with an abundance of faunal motifs.

LOCATION

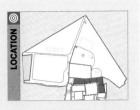

1

2

1

2

3

2

3

01 to 04. Garden of Troy. The architect Vermondo Resta tried for the first time in this space the aesthetic contrast of introducing unpolished stone blocks within the context of a perfectly plastered wall, a Mannerist resource that was used a few years later in the Grotto Gallery, in the same gardens of the Alcazar. **05 to 08. Dance Garden.** It is comprised of two areas situated on different levels, the first is presided over by two columns that used to finish in sculptures of dancing mythological beings –hence the garden's name– and the second, lower down, by a paved walkway endowed with diverse *burladores* small holes in the ground that shoot jets of water up by surprise). The fountain in the centre of the walkway dates back to the 16th century.

The Pond Garden

The pond and the Almohad walls lose their functional purpose in order to have a recreational use.

Pond railing
The pedestals are adorned with heraldic lion figures and dolphins that play with spheres, from the C16th.

The former palace cistern

The pond that gives its name to the garden to the east of the Gothic Palace is the primitive reservoir that received the water coming from the *Caños de Carmona*, the Roman aqueduct that furnished the palace and city with water. In 1575 it lost its function and converted into a purely decorative pond, which was when the central fountain, the bronze sculpted figure of Mercury, was put into place. In 1612 the Italian Vermondo Resta built over the pond's western wall the so-called Upper Viewpoint, an arcaded gallery with semi-circular arches.

Panel over the pond
The historian José Gestoso, author of many modern tile panels in the Alcazar, did this one with the royal coat of arms, at the end of the 19th century.

 1

The pond
It used to collect the water arriving by means of some pipes set in the wall, next to the road which is now known as the 'Alleyway of Water' *(Callejón del Agua)*.

 2

Caduceus
Mercury's attribute is a bar with two snakes.

 3

Winged sandals

Winged helmet

Bronze sculpture

The paintings
Frescos of mythological theme on the first archways of the gallery were painted at the start of the 17th century and roughly restored in the 20th.

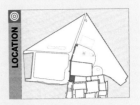

Mercury
The God of trade symbolizes the wealth of Seville as mercantile port.

1912

IS THE YEAR
in which the *Caños de Carmona*, the Roman aqueduct was demolished.

Pinnacle
Top of the arch situated in the upper level of the start of the Grotto Gallery.

The Grotto Gallery

Stemming from the Pond Garden is the wall that originally made up the stretch built in the 12th century by the Almohads and that Vermondo Resta converted between 1612 and 1621 into the Grotto Gallery, a blend of polished and rocky stones of marked Mannerist character that starts, at the height of the pond, with blind semicircular arches with frescos and continues as an arcaded gallery down the length of the Damsels' Garden and the Alcove Garden, on one side, and the Retreat and Poets', on the other.

160

METRES
Is the length of the Grotto Gallery, from its beginning next to the northern wall of the Pond Garden to its finish on an angle in the Alcove Garden.

The gallery
After the first stretch of blind arches, the gallery opens up on both sides of the gardens: the Damsels' to the west and the Retreat to the east.

Termination in angle
The rocky Grotto Gallery closes with a short stretch on a right angle, at one end of the Alcove Garden.

Rustic labour
Vermondo Resta combined stone without even smoothing down carved ashlars, a resource that appears in Mannerist architectonic techniques of the period.

The Damsels' Garden

For size and monumentality, it is the most important legacy of Mannerist architect Vermondo Resta.

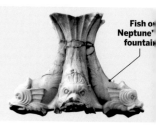

Fish o
Neptune'
fountai

Royal privacy

Towards the end of the 16th century, the Damsels' Garden only took up a small portion of its present size, in the section of the Alcazar's orchard nearest to the palace, close to the historic gardens. For this reason, workers and visitors to the neighbouring garden could see and even hear the people in the palace's windows, galleries and gardens, a fact that made its inhabitants somewhat uneasy. To guarantee privacy of the royal family and its guests, Vermondo Resta was commissioned with an enlargement of the Damsels' Garden that would mean they could stroll around without being observed by strangers.

1606
IS THE YEAR in which Vermondo Resta receives the commission to plan and enlarge the Damsels' Garden.

<<<
Neptune
The monumental fountain on the main thoroughfare of the Damsels' Garden is presided by a sculpture of Neptune carved in Genoa, whose dynamic posture emulates those of Italian Renaissance sculptor Giovanni da Bologna.

Trident

Railing. It borders the Alcove Garden, in the area formerly occupied by the Alcazar's Muslim garden.

Door. Located just in front of the entrance to the María Padilla Baths, it connects with the Dance Garden.

Fountain
As well as the monumental fountain dedicated to Neptune, the Damsels' Garden has other fountains with sculptural work.

Decoration of the walls
Vermondo Resta decorated the doors, walls and garden railings with Mannerist pinnacles of rounded form.

LOCATION

8
BEDS
of myrtle bushes are part of the landscaping of the Damsels' Garden.

4000
METRES SQUARE
is the surface area of the Damsels', situated between the historic gardens and the Alcove Garden.

The garden
The "damsels" are Goddesses Hera, Atenea and Aphrodite, and Queen Helena, whose sculptures, now gone, decorated the Fountain of Fame.

Mythical iconography

Vermondo Resta took advantage of the enlargement of the garden to start a complete transformation of the area. The architect devised a large space enclosed by walls and railings, and divided its rectangular shape into eight beds of myrtle bushes by a central passage with various lined up fountains and multiple jet fountains, which spurt out water from the paving and form arches of water. In line with the mythological iconography that shows his mark in the gardens, Resta decorated the most monumental of these fountains with a sculpture of Neptune and designed natural grottos on four points of the walls, while putting sculptures of Hellenistic themes opposite them.

NOTE
FOUNTAIN OF FAME

An aquatic organ
Vermondo Resta devised a monumental fountain on the wing of the garden that borders with the Grotto Gallery. Endowed with caryatids (1), Hermes (2) and a mechanism that made organ pipes sound with the flow of the water, the fountain got its name from the figure that tops the sculpture (3).

The Alcove Garden

The Charles V Pavilion is the jewel of the central sector of the former Muslim orchard of the Alcazar.

Lion fountain
Five sculpted faces with spouts in mouths regurgitate water into the pond that is in front of the Lion's Bower.

The Charles V Pavilion

The oldest building of the gardens is the Charles V Pavilion or the Alcove Bower, so-called for its origin as *qubba* or Muslim oratory. This construction, which gave its name to all the Alcazar orchard, was restored between 1543 and 1546 in order to be converted into a pavilion for relaxation dedicated to Charles V, who was in his final years of reign. In its cubed and arcaded configuration, with its hipped roof, Muslim ornaments and structures are combined, Mudejar and plateresque, generating a space full of harmony and balance in which stand out ceramic paving stones of geometric design, the fountain that brings freshness and relaxation, the very high skirting boards of floral tiles and the severe roof of wooden coffers.

Charles V Pavilion
All its walls are covered with tiles from the *Triana* neighbourhood and topped with plasterwork, plateresque inside and Mudejar on the outside.

4100
METRES SQUARE
is the area of the Alcove Garden, in the centre of the Alcazar's gardens.

The Privilege Doorway
The shapes of this door are inspired by the drawings of Italian architect Vignola, father of Mannerism.

 NOTE
THE LION BOWER

Tiled cupola
In 1645 to the south of the Charles V Pavilion another pavilion was built, called the Lion Bower for the sculpture (3) opposite its pond (1). The bower, whose walls were painted in fresco, is topped by a tiled cupola and holds a fountain (2).

The columns of Charles V's Pavilion
Carved in marble by Genoese artists, they are on top of benches decorated with tilework.

Door leading to the Damsels' Garden
This Mannerist arch connects the Alcove Garden with its western neighbour.

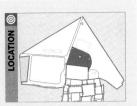

LOCATION

1991
IS THE YEAR
in which a restoration of the Lion Bower brings to light the frescos that covered its walls.

General view
The palm trees planted in the 19th century. tower above.

The Privilege Doorway

The eastern wing of the garden borders with the end of the Grotto Gallery, on whose wall Vermondo Resta planned the Privilege Doorway, a monumental entrance of three levels with a semicircular arch shape that opens on to the New Gardens and is inspired by models by Italian Vignola.

Marquis' Garden of Retreat

The site to the east of the Grotto Gallery was one of the last sectors of the orchard that were landscaped.

Ceramic urn
They decorate some pedestals of the Marquis' Garden of Retreat.

The Sevillian garden

The eastern half of the Alcazar gardens is taken up by the so-called New Gardens, divided into two by the Royal Way (*Camino Real*) that leads outside the palace's boundaries through the Countryside Door. To the north of this way the Marquis' Garden of Retreat was built between 1913 and 1917, in the former location of the garden with the same name. This space, one of the largest of the Alcazar's gardens, emulates the grid of hedges of the Damsels' Garden, situated right behind the Grotto Gallery, following the directives of what at the start of the twentieth century was called the *jardín sevillano*, a combination of Mannerist structures and Andalusian details, such as the channels that go along the paths between fountains and the tiled benches.

1,6

HECTARES
is the surface area of the Garden of Retreat, situated to the east of the Palace of Peter I.

1

Alfonso XIII
Coat of arms, with the kings initial on the irises, symbol of the Borbones, on the garden benches.

2

Fountains
Intersections between the different avenues of the grid form squares adorned with fountains in the centre.

3

Perspectives
The large area of the garden allows that its paths form perspectives with the hedge and cypress trees.

4

Fountain and channel
Naturalist fountain whose spring forms a canal decorated with tiles of geometric shape of Andalusian style.

Coats of arms on the ground
A cross which is decorated with the symbols of Castile and León decorates the composition of paving tiles.

The fountains
Fountains of different forms line up in the garden passages, some of them connected to each other by channels.

LOCATION

01 to 04. The Poets' Garden. Situated in the New Gardens, behind the Privilege Doorway, it was the last to be planned (1956-1958). It is inspired by the Sevillian park of María Luisa and includes two large pools surrounded by hedges. **05. Almohad tower, English Garden.** Of the 12th century, it is the oldest trace of the gardens after the Charles V Pavilion. It topped the stretch of wall that later converted into the Grotto Gallery. **06. Maze.** Created in 1914 using hedges, it tried to copy the Blind Labyrinth that had disappeared four years before the remodelling of the Cross Garden, situated to the west of the Alcazar. **07. The Cross Garden.** It holds the so-called Monte Parnaso, a natural grotto whose interior hides a sculpture of nymphs.

VISUAL GUIDE TO THE ROYAL ALCAZAR OF SEVILLE

PUBLISHED BY
© DOS DE ARTE EDICIONES, S.L., BARCELONA, 2010.

TEXTS
MANAGING DIRECTORS:
CARLOS GIORDANO AND NICOLÁS PALMISANO
REDACTION: RICARD REGÀS.
TRANSLATIONS:
CERYS GIORDANO JONES AND DYLAN GIORDANO JONES
© DOS DE ARTE EDICIONES, S.L., BARCELONA, 2010.

PHOTOGRAPHS
AUTHORS: CARLOS GIORDANO AND NICOLÁS PALMISANO
© DOS DE ARTE EDICIONES, S.L., BARCELONA, 2010.

ILLUSTRATIONS
AUTHORS: CARLOS GIORDANO AND NICOLÁS PALMISANO
© DOS DE ARTE EDICIONES, S.L., BARCELONA, 2010.

WITH THE FOLLOWING EXCEPTIONS:
• PAGE 14. PAINTING: VIEW OF SEVILLE BY ALFONSO SÁNCHEZ
  COELLO. MUSEUM OF AMERICA.
• PAGES: 004, 008, 009, 010, 013, 015, 016, 027, 033, 036, 041 AND
  083. ALL OF THEM PORTRAITS EXCEPT FOR PAGE 004.
  AUTHOR: ENRIQUE TORTOSA DEL TORO.
© DOS DE ARTE EDICIONES, S.L., BARCELONA, 2010.
• PAGES: 008 (MAP), 009 (MAP), 010 (MAP + WISE KING), 011
  (CONQUEST), 013 (CHRONOLOGY), 014 (MAP AND BOAT), 015
  (SHIELD AND CHRONOLOGY), 017 (BOOK AND ISABEL II) AND
  036 (DATA).
  AUTHOR: GABRIEL OREGIONI - COMPAÑÍA GRÁFICA.
© DOS DE ARTE EDICIONES, S.L., BARCELONA, 2010.
• PAGE 036. PAINTING: ALEJO FERNÁNDEZ.
• PAGE 082. TAPESTRY WORK: GUILLERMO PANNEMAKER.

ACKNOWLEDGMENTS
MANUEL HURTADO - REAL ALCÁZAR DE SEVILLA

SECOND EDITION 2010

ISBN
978-84-96783-51-5

DEPÓSITO LEGAL
B-27.518-09

PRINTED IN SPAIN

DOSᴅᴇ arTe
EDICIONES

www.dosdearte.com
info@dosdearte.com

DOWNLOAD

Extra Content!
www.dosdearte.com

This book contains a code that
enables you to download
an **extra chapter** from
our website

Using the code you will be
able to download extra material, visiting the "Download
zone" on our web page.

THT2041HTH

THE TEXTS IN THIS BOOK HAVE BEEN
WRITTEN WITH THE COLLABORATION OF:

R.A.
PATRONATO DEL REAL ALCÁZAR DE SEVILLA

THIS BOOK CONTAINS RELIABLE
INFORMATION CORROBORATED BY THE ROYAL
ALCAZAR OF SEVILLE FOUNDATION.